MUNSON MONUMENT.  STATE MONUMENT.

# INDIAN MASSACRE

and

# CAPTIVITY OF HALL GIRLS

## COMPLETE HISTORY

of the

## MASSACRE OF SIXTEEN WHITES

on

INDIAN CREEK, NEAR OTTAWA, ILL.

and

## SYLVIA HALL AND RACHEL HALL

As Captives in Illinois and Wisconsin

during

THE BLACK HAWK WAR, 1832

BY

## CHARLES M. SCANLAN

Author of
"Scanlan's Rules of Order," "The Law of Church and Grave,"
"Law of Hotels" Etc.

HERITAGE BOOKS
2007

# HERITAGE BOOKS
*AN IMPRINT OF HERITAGE BOOKS, INC.*

Books, CDs, and more—Worldwide

For our listing of thousands of titles see our website
at
www.HeritageBooks.com

A Facsimile Reprint
Published 2006 by
HERITAGE BOOKS, INC.
Publishing Division
65 East Main Street
Westminster, Maryland 21157-5026

Copyright © 1915 Charles M. Scanlan

— Publisher's Notice —
In reprints such as this, it is often not possible to remove blemishes from the original. We feel the contents of this book warrant its reissue despite these blemishes and hope you will agree and read it with pleasure.

International Standard Book Number: 978-0-7884-2177-8

PREFACE.

No one is satisfied with an incomplete story. The very meagre and inconsistent accounts of the adventures of Sylvia and Rachel Hall (familiarly known as the "Hall girls") heretofore published, merely excited one's curiosity to know the whole story. The ladies' statements that have been published, gave only an outline of the facts as far as they knew them personally. To obtain all the facts, required much investigation of books and a great deal of correspondence with historical societies, editors of newspapers and the War and the Interior Department of the United States. Also, the writer has had personal interviews with relatives of the Misses Hall, and has traveled over the ground and examined all the evidence that now appears from the location of the little cottage on Indian Creek to Galena where the girls took a boat for St. Louis.

Mrs. A. Miranda Dunavan, a daughter of Mrs. Rachel Hall Munson (the younger captive), gave me the family history of her mother; and Miss Sylvia E. Horn of Lincoln, Nebraska, and Mr. C. L. Horn of Mackinaw, Illinois, grand-children of Mrs. Sylvia Hall Horn (the elder captive), contributed the history of the Horn family. Thus every fact in the following pages is stated upon the best evidence.

To gather all the traditions that still linger along the course over which the Indians traveled with their captives, the writer enlisted the services of his nieces, Miss Gertrude Scanlan of Fennimore, Wisconsin, and Miss Marian Scanlan of Prairie du Chien, whose grandfathers were pioneers in the lead regions. However, no fact has been stated on tradition without the clues being verified by land records or government documents.

Of course every lady wants to know how the girls looked. Unfortunately, there is no picture of either of them prior to middle life. Mrs. Dunavan lent to me a very rare daguerreotype picture of her mother, Mrs. Munson, taken at the age of about forty-two years, and a photograph of her aunt, Mrs. Sylvia Hall Horn, taken when she was over sixty years of age. Also, I borrowed from Mrs. Dunavan a tintype picture of herself when she was sixteen, which is said to be a very good likeness of her aunt Sylvia at the time that she was taken captive. These pictures are reproduced herein. The tradition of the neighborhood is that the girls were unusually handsome in both figure and face and of captivating kind dispositions. They were born in Kentucky and carried with them to Illinois the southern culture which has won for the ladies of the South considerable fame in story and song.

> "She was bred in old Kentucky,
> Where the meadow grass grows blue,
> There's the sunshine of the country,
> In her face and manner too."—Braisted.

Milwaukee, Wis.
July 15, 1915.

CHARLES M. SCANLAN.

# CONTENTS

|      |                          | PAGE |
|------|--------------------------|------|
| Preface, |                      | 3    |
| I.   | Description of the Country, | 9 |
| II.  | Indian Davis Troubles,   | 13   |
| III. | The Davis Settlement,    | 23   |
| IV.  | The Massacre,            | 31   |
| V.   | The Captivity,           | 38   |
| VI.  | To the Rescue,           | 48   |
| VII. | Military Movements,      | 51   |
| VIII.| Reward Offered,          | 54   |
| IX.  | The Captive Girls,       | 59   |
| X.   | Ransomed,                | 66   |
| XI.  | Royally Welcomed,        | 81   |
| XII. | Homeward Bound,          | 90   |
| XIII.| Romance and History,     | 95   |
| XIV. | Shabona,                 | 106  |
| XV.  | Comee and Toquamee,      | 111  |

# CHAPTER I.
### DESCRIPTION OF THE COUNTRY.

In its natural condition, perhaps no more attractive country ever laid before the eyes of man than that in which occurred the incidents of the following narrative. On the south it is bordered by the Illinois river, with its historical events beginning with the old Kaskaskia Mission established by Father Marquette in 1673 amidst the most beautiful scenery in tne whole state of Illinois, which is now included in Starved Rock State Park.

What memories cluster around old Kaskaskia! As the first capital of Illinois, it was visited by Gen. La Fayette and Presidents Jackson, Lincoln, Taylor and Harrison; by Jefferson Davis, Gen. Albert Sidney Johnson, and by nearly every other man who was prominent in United States history prior to 1837, when Springfield became the state capital.

On the east for more than one hundred miles the Fox river, with its source in a beautiful lake near Waukesha, Wisconsin, flows south into the Illinois at Ottawa. Westward the great prairie stretches off to and beyond the Rock river which has eroded a narrow valley through that otherwise flat plain. Besides Rock river the only important streams that lay in the course of travel of the Hall girls as prisoners, were the Sycamore (South Kishwaukee) and the Kishwaukee in Illinois, and Turtle Creek, the Bark River and the Oconomowoc in Wisconsin.

We are told by geologists that during the quaternary age of the world, a great ice-berg, moving down from the north, crushed all the trees and vegetation in its path, leveled most of the hills and filled most of the valleys as far south as the Ohio River. When that body of ice melted it formed lakes in the depressions which were not filled with till. Drumlins, eskers and kames, here and there, remain to indicate either the resistance of the prior formation or that quantities of earth filled the uneven under surface of the ice at the time of its dissolution.

By the action of the atmosphere, rains and dew, as centuries rolled on, vegetation sprang up all over that great plain, and springs to supply the greatest necessity of living things, broke forth and flowed in streams that united into rivers as they rolled on to the sea. Along the streams were forests of trees—including many species of the oak, ash, sycamore, elm, sugar

A PRAIRIE FIRE—MC KENNEY.

maple, locust, hickory, walnut, butternut, linden, cherry, buckeye, blackberry and many other familiar varieties. Also, here and there stood groves that escaped the terrible prairie fires that almost every year swept over that vast plain.

Game of many kinds, from the monstrous buffalo and timid deer down to the rabbit, the turkey, the prairie chicken, and the quail, was abundant.

Last, and by no means least, was the beautiful flora of that country which was known as "The Paradise of the West."[1] A traveler who saw it in its natural condition, describes it as follows: "Above all countries, this is the land of flowers. In the season, every prairie is an immense flower garden. In the early stages of spring flowers, the prevalent tint is peach bluish; the next is a deeper red; then succeeds the yellow; and to the latest period of autumn the prairies exhibit a brilliant golden, scarlet and blue carpet, mingled with the green and brown ripened grass."[2]

> "Sweet waves the sea of summer flowers
> Around our wayside cot so coy,
> Where Eileen sings away the hours
> That light my task in Illinois."—McGee.

[1] 6 Wis. Hist. Col., 421; 10 Wis. Hist. Col., 246-7.
[2] "Western Portraiture," Colton, 221.

## CHAPTER II.

### INDIAN TROUBLES.

When the first white man settled in Illinois, the Mascoutin Indians occupied the lands between the Illinois River and the waterway formed by the Fox and Wisconsin Rivers from Green Bay to Prairie du Chien. Later the Sacs, the Foxes, and the Pottawatamies, occupied the territory and had many villages. There were no national boundary lines. A prominent route of travel was the Kishwaukee Trail from Watseca in Eastern Illinois up the Kankakee to where it flows into the Illinois, and thence in a northwesterly direction to the mouth of the Kishwaukee on Rock River, about six miles below Rockford. Dixon was the great center of trails. The principal one was from Kaskaskia by way of Dixon to Galena, Illinois. Numerous other trails connected prominent points and various Indian villages.

In 1804 a treaty was made with the Sacs and Foxes at St. Louis, of which the principal provision were as follows:

"Article 1. The United States receive the united Sac and Fox tribes into their friendship and protection and the said tribes agree to con-

[13]

sider themselves under the protection of the United States, and no other power whatsoever.

"Article 2. The General boundary line between the land of the United States and the said Indian tribes shall be as follows, to-wit: Beginning at a point on the Missouri River opposite to the mouth of the Gasconde River; thence, in a direct course so as to strike the River Jeffreon to the Mississippi; thence, up the Mississippi to the mouth of the Ouisconsing [Wisconsin] River, and up the same to a point which shall be 36 miles in a direct line from the mouth of the said river, thence, by a direct line to the point where the Fox River (a branch of the Illinois) leaves the small lake called Sakaegan; thence, down the Fox River to the Illinois River, and down the same to the Mississippi. And the said tribes, for and in consideration of the friendship and protection of the United States, which is now extended to them, of the goods (to the value of two thousand two hundred and thirty-four dollars and fifty cents) which are now delivered, and of the annuity hereinafter stipulated to be paid, do hereby cede and relinquish forever, to the United States, all the lands included within the above described boundary.

"Article 3. In consideration of the cession and relinquishment of land made in the preceding article, the United States will deliver to the said tribes, at the town of St. Louis, or some other convenient place on the Mississippi, yearly and every year, goods suited to the circumstances of the Indians of the value of one thousand dollars (six hundred of which are intended for the Sacs and four hundred for the Foxes), reckoning that value at the first cost of the goods in the City or place in the United States, where they shall be procured. And if the said tribes shall hereafter at an annual delivery of the goods aforesaid, desire that a part of their annuity should be furnished in domestic animals, implements of husbandry, and other utensils, convenient for them, or in compensation to useful artificers, who may reside with or near them, and be employed for their benefit, the same shall, at the subsequent annual delivery, be furnished accordingly.

"Article 4. The United States will never interrupt the said tribes in the possession of the lands, which they rightfully claim, but will, on the contrary, protect them in the quiet enjoyment of the same against their own citizens and against all other white persons, who may intrude upon them. And the said tribes do hereby engage that they will never sell their lands, or any part thereof, to any sovereign power but the United States, nor to the citizens or subjects of any other sovereign power, nor to the citizens of the United States.

\* \* \* \* \* \* \* \* \*

"Article 7. As long as the lands which are now ceded to the United States remain their [U. S.] property, the Indians belonging to the said tribes shall enjoy the privileges of living and hunting upon them."[3]

The Chippewas, the Winnebagos, and the Pottawatamies, made claim to the same territory. Even the Foxes and Sacs claimed that the young chiefs who signed the treaty, were made drunk, and while in that condition agreed to the treaty.[4] Also, the Indians maintained that the United States would not allow them to hunt upon the "wild" lands, notwithstanding Art. 7 of the treaty and that the title thereto was still in the government. Therefore, the Indians refused to ratify the treaty, and the idea that they were grievously wronged became a fixed notion in the minds of the old chiefs,

---

[3]2 "Indian Affairs, Laws and Treaties", 174.
[4]"Black Hawk's Autobiography, Le Claire, Ch. 3.
12 "The Republic", Irelan, 68.

BLACK HAWK AS A WARRIOR.

which led to the Red Bird War of 1827, and the still greater Black Hawk War in 1832.[5]

---

[3] Smith's "History of Wisconsin" (1854), 115 et seq.; "Waubun," Kinzie, 381.

Black Hawk had fought with the English in the War of 1812, and by reason of the defeat of the English, including his own, he retained his natural desire for revenge against the Americans. He was born at Rock Island, and had as strong love for his native place as was ever retained by any white man. When Illinois became a state in 1818, Black Hawk with all his people was ordered to move across the Mississippi into Iowa, which he reluctantly obeyed. However, he was never satisfied with his new location, and in 1832 he again crossed the Mississippi with four hundred warriors and all their squaws and children and squatted on his former possessions at Rock Island. He was ordered back to Iowa, but refused to go until he learned that troops were being sent against him. With all his people he retired north along Rock River, followed by the Illinois militia, and when he reached a point about twenty-five miles south of Rockford, he halted and held a council of war with chiefs of the Pottawatomies and Winnebagoes, where he delivered the following speech:

"I was born at the Sac Village, and here I spent my childhood, youth and manhood. I liked to look on this place with its surroundings of big rivers, shady groves and green prairies. Here are the graves of my father and some of my children. Here I expected to live and die and lay my bones beside those near and dear to me; but now in my old age I have been driven from my home, and dare not look again upon this loved spot."

The old chief choked with grief and tears flowed down his cheeks. Covering his face in his blanket, he remained silent for a few moments. Then wiping away his tears, he continued:

"Before many moons you, too, will be compelled to leave your homes. The haunts of your youth, your villages, your corn fields, and your hunting grounds, will be in the possession of the whites, and by them the graves of your fathers will be plowed up, while your people will be retreating towards the setting sun to find new homes beyond the Father of Waters. We have been as brothers; we fought side by side in the British war; we hunted together and slept under the same blanket; we have met at councils and at religious feasts; our people are alike and our interests are the same."[6]

On the 14th day of May, 1832, the militia

---
[6]Memories of Shaubena, 98.

under Major Stillman arrived within eight miles of the camp of a Black Hawk who sent three Indians under a flag of truce to negotiate a treaty with the whites. The wily chief also sent five other Indians to a point where they could watch the unarmed braves carrying the white flag. Stillman's men refusing to recognize the white flag set upon the Indians, killed one and captured the others, and then set off after the other five who held their guns crosswise over their heads as a sign of friendship. The whites killed two of the five and chased the others into Black Hawk's camp. Then the Indians set upon Stillman's army, cut it to pieces, and chased the scattered remnants for many miles. The place of that battle is known as "Stillman's Run."[7] The disgrace of the entire affair has been a dark blot upon the white man's bravery and his manner of dealing with the Indians. Up to this time the Indians had committed no crime nor act of war against the whites.[8]

Immediately after the engagement Black Hawk called another council of his braves, at

---

[7]"Life of Albert Sidney Johnston," Johnston, 35.
[8]12 Wis. Hist. Col., 230; "History of Indiana," Esarey, 323; "The Black Hawk War," 129-144.

BLACK HAWK AS A CIVILIAN.

which it was determined to fight to the last and to send out small bands of Indians to the various white settlements to destroy them. Among the great warriors present at that council was the celebrated Chief Shabona (Shab-eh-ney)[9] who fought beside Tecumseh at his down-fall at the battle of the Thames. Shabona pleaded with the Indian chiefs to give up the war and to return to Iowa, and when they refused to do so, he, his son Pypagee, and his nephew Pyps, mounted ponies and rode to the various white settlements and notified the people of the danger of the Indians. The first horse with which Shabona started, dropped dead under him; but he obtained another horse from a farmer and rode day and night until he had warned the whites at all the settlements.

"Lo, the poor Indian! whose untutored mind
 Sees God in the clouds, or hears Him in the wind."
—Pope.

---

[9] 7 Wis. Hist. Col., 323, 415; "The Black Hawk War," Stevens, 160.

## CHAPTER III.

### THE DAVIS SETTLEMENT.

The father of our heroines, William Hall, who was born in Georgia, migrated to Kentucky where he married Mary J. Wilburs, and in 1825 emigrated to Mackinaw, about fifteen miles south of Peoria, Illinois, where he opened a farm. Shortly afterwards he moved to the lead mines near Galena where he staid three years, and then returned to Lamoille, Bureau County, Illinois. In the spring of 1832 he sold out his mining claim and settled upon a homestead about two miles east of the farm of William Davis. Prior to that time his oldest daughter, Temperance, had been married to Peter Cartwright, but the other members of his family, consisting of his wife, three daughters— Sylvia, aged 19, Rachel, aged 17, and Elizabeth, aged 8 years, and two boys, were living with him. Some time prior to the massacre, two Indians named Co-mee and To-qua-mee, who had been frequent visitors at the Hall home and treated kindly by Mr. Hall's daughters, endeavored, after the custom of the Indians, to purchase Sylvia and Rachel from their father.[10]

---

[10]"The Black Hawk War," Stevens, 149.

## THE DAVIS SETTLEMENT.

MRS. DUNAVAN, AGED 16, LIKENESS OF SYLVIA HALL.

The Halls were noted for their hospitality. Judge Edwin Jerome of Detroit relates that he was the guest of the family one night in April 1832.[11]

William Petigrew, also from Kentucky, who had just migrated to the Davis Settlement and had not yet established a home for himself, with his wife and two children, was temporarily stopping at the home of Mr. Davis at the time of the massacre.

---

[11] 1 "Michigan Pioneers", Jerome, 49.

## THE DAVIS SETTLEMENT. 25

In 1830, John H. Henderson emigrated from Tennessee to Indian Creek and settled on a homestead adjoining the land of Davis on the south. Subsequently the Hendersons became prominent politicians, both in Illinois and Iowa. In the spring of 1830, William Davis, a Kentuckian, and a blacksmith by trade, settled on a land claim on Big Indian Creek, twelve miles north of Ottowa, in the northern part of La Salle County, Illinois. He was the first white settler at that place.

Agriculture and marriage have always been the great necessities to found permanent civilization. To establish a settlement in the great west, at that time, a blacksmith shop and a mill were the next two great necessities, and around those the early settlers broke up the wild prairie and on the upturned sod sowed buckwheat, turnips and sod-corn, which within three months produced their first food from the soil for themselves and their stock. To "break" the tough prairie sod required a sharp plowshare and colter, which had to be resharpened frequently. Without the blacksmith the prairie could hardly be cultivated. The big ox-teams of the neighbors, with which they had moved into the country, pulled the plow. Next, with the crop produced, the grist mill to grind the grain was a great necessity. The Indians and some of the early settlers with hammers and stones pulverized corn and wheat enough to supply their absolute wants from day to day, but the whites, who had been accustomed to corn-meal and wheat-flour bread, were not satisfied with the mashed product. Therefore, Davis, who supplied both of those great necessities, was a prominent man in the Davis Settlement.

The mill-site was where the Sauk trail from Black Hawk's Village at the mouth of the Rock River crossed Big Indian Creek and continued thence east to Canada, where the whole tribe of Sacs went every year to get their annuities from the English Government.[12] Just above the ford the creek meandered through a flat-bottomed gulch that was about two hundred feet wide with precipitous banks about fifteen feet high. At this point the stream flowed southeasterly and was fringed along its course with woods that grew dense, and here and there expanded into groves, but at other places there were openings where the prairie fires annually destroyed the undergrowth and left standing

---

[12]Blanchard's History of Illinois, 122, and Historical Map.

SHABONA PARK, SHOWING MILL POND AND MONUMENT.

only the monarchs of the forest. The north bank of the gulch had an incline of about forty-five degrees to the level of the prairie. On that bank in a sparsely timbered opening from which the prairie stretched off to the cardinal points of the compass, William Davis located his home and erected his cabin. About that cabin there were trees that produced fruit, fuel and lumber, among whose branches were singing birds of great variety, including the Cardinal, the Dickcissel, the Carolina Wren, the Thrush and the Robin. By May the bank was covered with a carpet of thick, waving grass, diversified with ever-changing colored flowers, until the cruel frost of Fall destroyed them. It was an idyllic spot. No doubt Davis hoped that some day the Davis Settlement would become Davis City, and that his generations would revel in mansions that would replace the cottage on the bank of that new Jordan, where he, like King David, in his old age might kneel among his people to pray.

However, the hopes and aspirations of the Davis family were soon to be blasted. Davis was a powerful man and his Kentucky blood fairly boiled with resentment at any offense, particularly one given by an Indian, upon whom

## THE DAVIS SETTLEMENT.

he looked as an inferior. With his gun and bowie knife Davis would fight a dozen Indians —aye, a score. It seemed as though he could play with them in the air as an athlete plays with Indian clubs.

About one hundred and fifty feet south of his cottage, Davis erected a blacksmith shop and a mill. To obtain water power for his mill it became necessary for Davis to put a dam across the stream. Six miles farther up Indian Creek there was an Indian village, and as the fish naturally went up the stream every spring, there was good fishing at the village for the Indians. The dam prevented the fish from going up, and the Indians protested against this invasion of their rights. Davis, however, insisted on his rights to build and maintain the dam, and bad feelings were engendered.

One day in April, 1832, Davis discovered an Indian tearing an outlet in the dam, and with a hickory stick he beat the Indian unmercifully.[13] Had he killed the Indian it might have ended the affair; but to whip an Indian with a stick as you would whip a dog, was an insult that incurred the resentment of the whole Indian village, and instilled in the Indian a rank-

---
[13]Black Hawk's Autobiography, Le Claire, Ch. XII.

CHIEF SHABONA.

ling desire for revenge. The incident, however, was settled by Chief Shabona with the assistance of another Indian chief named Waubansee, who advised the Indians not to resort to forceful reparation and to do their fishing below the dam. The Indians followed Shabona's advice for some time, but after a while Davis noticed that they ceased to go below the dam to fish, and being quite familiar with the Indian character, he took it as an intimation of their anger, and he prepared for hostilities.

## CHAPTER IV.

### THE MASSACRE.

The year 1831 was known to early settlers in Illinois as "The Dry Year." There was little rain and there were long spells of great heat, so that vegetation was parched and the crop a failure. The season of 1832 was just the opposite.[14] During the first half of the month of May there were numerous heavy thunder storms with intervals of hot weather that made the grass and flowers grow very rapidly, but delayed the farmers in their planting. Also, the several Indian scares interrupted the settlers in their regular work in the fields.

As already stated, immediately after the breaking up of the Indian council after the defeat of Stillman, Shabona rode in post haste to the Davis Settlement and warned the people of the danger of an Indian massacre. The whites loaded on their wagons such articles as could be readily handled, and drove to Ottawa, the nearest fort, where there was a garrison of soldiers.

The Indians did not make the expected raid, and slowly the settlers returned to their home-

---

[14]"Historic Illinois," Parish, 258.

## THE MASSACRE.

steads. During this retreat some of the people tantalized Davis for running away from the Indians, and his reply was that he would never do so again.

On Monday morning, May 21st, Shabona again rode to the Davis Settlement and warned the whites that there was immediate danger of a massacre. At this time it happened that Davis was at Ottawa on some business when Shabona called. However, his family, and the neighbors hastily loaded their furniture and other movable articles on wagons, and hurriedly drove off to Ottawa. They had almost reached the fort when they met Davis, who ordered his own family to return, and urged the return of his immediate neighbors, inviting them all to go to his place where they would be perfectly safe. The Halls, Hendersons and Pettigrews, with two farm hands named Henry George and Robert Norris, reluctantly returned with Davis, and arrived at his cottage about noon.

After dinner John W. Henderson, Alexander Davis and a younger son of William Davis, Edward and Greenbury Hall, and Allen Howard, went to a field about one hundred rods south of the Davis cottage, to plant corn. In the middle of the afternoon William Hall, John W. Hall,

## THE MASSACRE.

Robert Norris, Henry George and William Davis, Jr., who were working on the mill-dam, gathered into the blacksmith shop where Davis was repairing his gun, to get a drink from a pail of water which had been brought from a nearby spring. All the loaded guns and the ammunition were in the dwelling house, where Pettigrew, with his baby in his arms, was chatting with the ladies who were sewing by the open door. The afternoon was very hot and was not inspiring to great exertion. The furniture which had been loaded to drive to Ottawa, was still on the wagons that stood in the yard. The perfume of the blooming flowers filled the air which was rich in its freshness after the many days of rain and lightning. All nature seemed to instil in the little Davis Settlement a feeling of safety or at least to relieve them from alarm during the daytime. With the coming darkness, no doubt, they would have all gathered into the little cottage and some of the men would have stood guard with their guns to watch for Indians.

About four o'clock a party of sixty to seventy Indians suddenly leaped over the garden fence, filled the yard, and part of them rushed towards the house. Mr. Pettigrew leaped forward to close the door, but was instantly shot dead. Through the open door the Indians rushed with spears, and hatchets, and guns, filling the little cottage. There was no place to hide and no chance for the whites to escape. In her despair Mrs. Pettigrew threw her arms around Rachel Hall and was killed by a shot so close to Rachel as to blacken her face with the powder. Rachel jumped upon the bed, which only placed her in view of more Indians and increased the danger of being shot.

The piteous screams of the women and children were terrifying. The Indians stuck them with spears and hacked them with tomahawks without feeling or mercy, and as they fell each victim's scalp was cut off with a big knife.

An Indian grabbed Pettigrew's baby by the legs, rushed out doors, swung the child over his head, and dashed its brains out against a stump in the yard. There, also, an Indian on each side held the youngest Davis boy by his hands, the little lad standing pale and silent, and a third Indian shot him dead. As his limp body fell, an Indian scalped him.

In a few moments all the whites in the house excepting Sylvia and Rachel Hall, namely: Mrs.

Wm. Hall, aged forty-five years, her daughter Elizabeth, aged eight years, Wm. Pettigrew, his wife and two children, and Mrs. Wm. Davis and her five children, were killed.

The sudden appearance of the Indians bewildered the men who were in the blacksmith shop, as they were cut off from their guns and ammunition. Young Davis slipped behind the shop and thence escaped down the creek. The others rushed towards the house and were met by a volley of shots. William Hall, whose breast was pierced by two bullets, with a prayer on his lips, fell dead at his son John's feet. Davis called out to John Hall to "Take care!" and then tried to escape to the woods. Notwithstanding his prowess and that he made a desperate fight for his life by using his unloaded gun as a club, he was in a short time so overcome by Indian warriors with their spears and tomahawks that with innumerable wounds he sank dead in his yard. John Hall was so paralyzed by the awful carnage, that for a moment he did not move from where his father lay. He watched the Indians reloading their guns, then as a man awakening from a night-mare he jumped down the high bank and a volley of bullets passed over

## 36          THE MASSACRE.

his head. By hugging closely to the bank next the Indians, he scrambled hastily down the stream and then ran as he never ran before, thus escaping. Norris and George slid down the bank and attempted to cross the creek, but a volley of bullets from the Indians killed one of them as he was climbing the bank, his body falling back into the creek, and the other fell on the green sward above.

John W. Henderson, two sons of Wm. Davis and two sons of Wm. Hall, who were at work in the cornfield when the Indians made the attack upon the Davis cottage, comprehending the situation, hastily fled to Ottawa. They had sped only about two miles when John W. Hall overtook them. By reason of his scudding from death in the great heat and his excited condition, John's account of the massacre was incoherently told with uncontrolled emotions of grief and rage. Believing that the Indians were pursuing, he did not check his speed, but urged the others to extra efforts until they reached the fort.

Sylvia and Rachel Hall were each seized by two Indians who dragged them out of the cottage to the yard where the final acts of the massacre were taking place.

In their fiendish desire for revenge for Stillman's treachery and to terrify the whites, the Indians cut out the hearts of some of the slain and otherwise mutilated their bodies. Of all the whites none but Rachel and Sylvia Hall remained alive to witness the closing act of the horrible tragedy. As they saw scattered in the yard the bodies of their murdered parents, their sister, and their neighbors—sixteen in all, the girls were stupefied with horror. The wonder is that the shock did not kill both of them.

The massacre has been described so often, and is so sickening in its particulars, that we drop the curtain on the tragic scene.[15]

[15] 3 Smith's "History of Wisconsin", 187; "History of La Salle County," Baldwin, 95; "The Black Hawk War," Stevens, 150; "Memories of Shabona," Matson, 145-155; *Ottawa Journal*, Aug. 30, 1906; 12 Transactions Ill. State Hist. Soc., 332; Ford's History of Illinois, 122.

## CHAPTER V.

### THE CAPTIVITY.

A person never knows what he would do under conditions and circumstances never before experienced: a mother who would flee from a cow, would, to protect her child, fight a tiger without thought of her own safety; a timid deer that would flee from a baby, when its nature is changed by a serious wound will fight a hunter to death; a soldier's nature becomes so changed in battle that he obeys orders like an automatom, and in his efforts to kill men exerts himself until the sweat rolls down his face as it would down the face of a harvest hand mowing grass.

Sylvia and Rachel Hall, who in the peace of their home would faint at the sight of blood, had their nature so changed during the slaughter and mutilation of their dear relatives and friends that they viewed the scene with horror that almost paralyzed them and put them in a psychological condition of mental aberration.

The spell of lethargy was rudely broken when the girls were dragged off as captives, first to the creek, and, after Rachel had been pulled half way across the stream, then back again to

THE CAPTIVITY. 39

the yard. There two Indians, each seizing one of Sylvia's hands, and two others taking Rachel in a similar manner, hustled the girls northward along the easterly side of the creek. The girls were soon in unknown lands through which they were tugged on, and on, not knowing whither nor to what fate. Did they cry? Of course they did; strong men would have wept under similar circumstances. Did they pray? Yes; but their prayers were not like the Pharisee's: they prayed with an intense feeling from the bottom of their hearts and with all the power of their souls. Were their prayers answered? Were they? Read on, read on!

After being hustled and half dragged about a mile and a half, they came to where a number of horses were tied in the edge of a grove. Here they met friends: horses belonging to their father and their neighbors. The horses pricked up their ears, looked at the girls and whinnied—returning the girls' recognition. If the girls could have mounted two of these friendly animals that were bred in Kentucky they might have ridden to freedom; but it was not so to be.

The Indians put each girl on a pony furnished with an Indian saddle and led by a warrior. Thus they traveled on, keeping due north.

After the sun had set the additional terror of darkness was enveloping them. Occasionally a night-hawk would break the awful silence by swooping down from his great height with his accustomed "Boo-oo-oo," and a whippoor-will would add his monotonous whistle from a decayed log in the adjacent woods. Otherwise, it was as solemn a procession as ever moved to the grave, and only for the crack of his whip and an occasional "ugh" from an Indian there was little to attract attention until they passed a large grove on their left. The girls had heard of Shabbona's Grove. Was this that historical sylvan place? Would Shabona come to their relief? He had saved them and their friends before, and if it had not been for the obstinacy of Davis they would not have been in their awful predicament. But the chief, worn out and tired from his long wild ride of the night before and asleep in his tent, was unconscious of the passing of that strange and unusual procession.

Hour after hour passed as the girls rode along weary and heart-sick on that dark night, with nothing but the stars to light their way, and not a ray of hope in their hearts. The head waters of Indian creek and of the Somonauk had been

## THE CAPTIVITY.                           41

passed and the source of the Sycamore was reached just as the moon was rising, 51 minutes after twelve o'clock.[16] Here the first stop was made and the girls were allowed to rest on some blankets on which they sat together, not daring to lie down to sleep. The Indians holding their ponies by the bridles, danced a little, but nothing was said that would indicate their intent, either as to the place of destination or what they intended to do with their captives. As the girls could not speak the Indian language or understand it, there was little medium of communication between them and the Indians. Their feelings of sorrow for their murdered relatives mixed with the uncertainty of their own fate, and their disheveled hair and soiled cheeks through which their tears washed courses, make them objects of woeful misery. Oh! if the girls could only wash their faces, which were stained with powder and the blood of their dear friends, or even in their sorrow comb each other's hair as they had often done at their father's cottage, it would have refreshed them, and, to some extent, relieved their distress.

---

[16]Washington Observatory Record; "Old Farmer's Almanac," 1832.

About half-past three o'clock in the morning of May 22nd, the girls were replaced on the ponies, the Indians remounted, and once more the train proceeded in its former order, with Indians before, on the sides, and in the rear of the girls. They passed groves, here and there, and hour after hour, with tiresome monotony, they moved along.

After the sun had lapped the dew, it grew very warm and Rachel became weary almost to collapse. She thought that if she could walk for a little while it would give her relief, notwithstanding her weak condition from fasting and worry. She did not know the language of the Indians, but necessity finds a way: she made signs of distress and indicated that she wanted to walk. The Indians understood her and assisted her from her pony. This little act of gallantry gave her the first indication of their human sympathy and inspired her with some confidence in their honor.

Limp and staggering, she managed to keep pace with the procession. When they reached the Kishwaukee there was no hesitation and all plunged into the stream. Rachel, who had not been replaced on her pony, was forced to wade across through water three feet deep.

## THE CAPTIVITY.

It was now about two o'clock in the afternoon and a stop was made about twenty-five miles easterly from Stillman's Run, on the west of a large grove, to allow the ponies to graze on the bank of the river. Here they remained for about two hours. The Indians scalded some beans and roasted some acorns, of which they ate heartily and offered portions to the girls, who tried to eat so as not to offend the Indians.

After the Indians had finished their lunch they busied themselves in stretching on little hoops the scalps that they had taken in the massacre at Indian Creek. The girls immediately recognized the scalps of some of their friends, particularly the scalp of their mother. The sight caused Sylvia to faint. Limp and unconscious she lay beside her sister, who by the incident was again put into her former psychic condition, being oblivious to everything about her excepting her sister's care. The subconscious thought that she had to protect Sylvia inspired her with superhuman strength as well as the fighting spirit of a lioness. If Sylvia should die! what then? If she should be unable to travel, would the Indians kill her? What torture of mind Rachel must have suffered!

About four o'clock Sylvia regained her consciousness, to the great relief of Rachel who recovered her normal condition of mind. By this time the Indians had gathered their horses, and replacing the girls on the ponies that they had been riding, all moved forward leisurely.

Shortly after starting a detachment of the Indians was sent out to scout to the westward, and after being gone some time they returned apparently excited, and immediately the procession assumed a double-quick, during which the Indian guards in the rear held their spears poised, as though they expected an attack. After traveling in that manner for about five miles, the Indians resumed their composure and slackened their speed to a walking pace.

Had the Indians seen some of Gen. Whiteside's scouts? Had they learned that a detachment of Illinois Militia, of which Abraham Lincoln was a member, was moving towards them up the Kishwaukee?[17] Or, were the Indians pursued by the friends of the girls?

If the whites should attack the Indians, Sylvia and Rachel feared that they would share the fate of their relatives and friends at the Davis Settlement. Therefore, when the excitement of

---
[17]XII Wis. Hist. Col., 241, 242; "The Black Hawk War." 146.

## THE CAPTIVITY. 45

the Indians subsided, a feeling of relief from danger of immediate death calmed the girls.

The extra exertion during the scare caused the pony that Sylvia was riding to give out, and it was abandoned. Sylvia was then placed behind an Indian on a fine horse belonging to Mr. Henderson, which, like the girls, had been taken captive at Indian Creek. Thus they traveled, on and on, until about nine o'clock in the evening when they arrived at Black Hawk's Grove on the east side of the present city of Janesville, Wisconsin, where the whole of Black Hawk's tribe was encamped.[18] During twenty-eight hours the girls had traveled about eighty miles from the place of their capture, and were worn out almost beyond description. No one can fully comprehend their condition without reflecting upon that extremely long ride on horseback, without food or drink, mourning their dead, and tortured with the worry over their future fate.

On their arrival at Black Hawk's Grove there was great rejoicing at the Indian camp. Several squaws hurried to the girls, assisted them off their horses, and conducted them to the cen-

---

[18]Hist. of Rock Co., by Gurnsey & Willard, 19; 14 Wis. Hist. Col., 129; 6 Wis. Hist. Col., 422.

ter of the camp where they had prepared a comfortable place in the form of beds of animal skins and blankets. Also, the squaws brought in wooden bowls, parched corn, meal and maple-sugar mixed, which they invited the girls to eat. More through fear than appetite, the girls partook of the food, although it was disgusting to them.

The squaws requested the girls to throw on the fire particles of food and some tobacco which they handed them. The girls complied with the request of their dusky hosts, although they did not know for what purpose it was required. As a matter of fact, it was a common practice among the Indian tribes to make the offering of food and tobacco to their gods in case of escape from death or as thanks for some extraordinary good fortune.[19]

The squaws requested Sylvia and Rachel to lie down on separate beds, and then a squaw lay on each side of each of the girls, so that there was no chance for escape. Thus abed, they had a night of confused, disordered sleep, in which visions of their friends and the scenes of the massacre haunted them almost continually. The

---

[19]2 "Indian Tribes of U. S.", Drake, 68, 72; 6 Schoolcraft's, "History of Indian Tribes of the U. S.", 83, 88.

squaws endeavored to soothe the girls, but they could not take the place of that mother who in their childish nightmares would say to them: "My dears, say a prayer and try to sleep."

"But God is sweet.
  My mother told me so,
  When I knelt at her feet
    Long—so long—ago;
She clasped my hands in hers.
  Ah! me, that memory stirs
  My soul's profoundest deep—
    No wonder that I weep.
She clasped my hands and smiled,
Ah! then I was a child—
  I knew no harm—
  My mother's arm
Was flung around me; and I felt
That when I knelt
  To listen to my mother's prayer,
  God was with mother there.
Yea! "God is sweet!"
  She told me so;
  She never told me wrong;
And through my years of woe
Her whispers soft, and sad, and low,
  And sweet as Angel's song,
  Have floated like a dream.—Fr. Ryan.

## CHAPTER VI.

### TO THE RESCUE.

When John W. Hall arrived at Ottawa he did not know that his sisters had been taken prisoners, but he supposed that they had been massacred with the rest of the people at the Davis cottage. His first impulse was revenge, and he rushed wildly about, urging men to arm and go with him to the scene of the massacre. The spirit of adventure was rampant among the people at the time, and John soon found himself at the head of a considerable number of mounted men armed with all kinds of guns, who followed him like a mob, from Ottawa to the Davis Settlement.

On their way out they met some of the men who were defeated at Stillman's Run, returning to Ottawa. John endeavored to have these men accompany him to the Davis Settlement, but they had enough of Indian adventure, and instead of assisting John, discouraged the men with him from engaging in a fight with the Indians.

When John's squadron arrived at the Davis cottage there was presented an awful sight—thirteen murdered and mutilated bodies in and about the cottage, some hung on shambles like butchered pigs, just as they were left by the Indians. On the creek below the cottage were found the bodies of Norris and George where they fell from the bullets of the Indians. The absence of his sisters Rachel and Sylvia from among the dead, presented to John a new quandary. A careful search was made about the premises but no traces of the girls could be found.

After having seen the awful deaths of their fellow-whites, the men who accompanied John had their desire for adventure changed to a feeling of fear, which they tried to hide under the excuse that it would be impossible to proceed after the Indians without rations and tents.

The situation was a trying one for John. In vain did he appeal to the men to help him rescue his sisters. Not one would volunteer to go with him, and after burying all the dead in one grave in front of the little cottage, John and his squadron hastily returned to Ottawa.

In hopes of rescuing his sisters, John again recruited a force and obtained the necessaries to follow up the Indians. Early on the second day after the massacre, with about forty men and two days' rations, without any commissary,

John led his little army to the Davis Settlement and along the Indian trail until he lost it on the great prairie. He concluded that the Indians had taken the "Kishwaukee Trail" to where the Kishwaukee flows into the Rock River, and he followed that route until he arrived at his objective point without attaining his chief aim. Disappointed in not even getting any information of his sisters and in not finding further track of the Indians, and his rations having run out, John was again obliged to return with his troops to Ottawa for a fresh supply, when once more he started on a fruitless search for his sisters.

## CHAPTER VII.

### MILITARY MOVEMENTS.

When a remnant of Stillman's men returned to Dixon after an exciting ride of twenty-four miles from Stillman's Run, they reported that they had been attacked by thousands of Indians and that all the rest of the army had been massacred. The exaggerated report set a few of the men who had not been with Stillman, keen to fight; but it instilled into most of them a sense of home-sickness, and many of them requested to be excused from duty. Gen. Taylor immediately reported the situation to Gen. Atkinson, at Ottawa, and the latter ordered Generals Whiteside and Harney, who were in command of some United States regulars, to pursue the Indians.

When the troops arrived at Stillman's Run they found the bodies of thirteen soldiers and most of the deserted commissary which had included a barrel of whiskey that Black Hawk emptied on the ground. Black Hawk destroyed the wagons and everything else that could not be carried away, excepting a few boats that belonged to the Indians which were left on the river bank.

## 52 MILITARY MOVEMENTS.

As a matter of fact Black Hawk had only forty warriors with him at the time of the attack on him by Stillman's men, while Stillman had about three hundred men. At the time of the attack many of Stillman's men were under the influence of liquor and most of them in such a state of insubordination that they paid no attention to the orders of their officers. Thus they rushed into the camp of Black Hawk, and, as each was acting independently, it was but a short time until the Indians by their shots and yells had the militia scared crazy and on the run.[20]

On May 22nd, in accordance with Gen. Anderson's order, Gen. Whiteside took up and followed the Indian trail for thirty-six miles along the Kishwaukee and the Sycamore; but when the high prairie was reached, the Indians scattered so in all directions that the troops were unable to track them further, and the army proceeded to the Fox River and down that stream to Ottawa, where it arrived on May 27th.

On the day that the girls passed a few miles to the east, the United States troops found on the Sycamore, articles belonging to the Indians

---

[20] The Black Hawk War, Stevens, 133, 137.

who committed the massacre at Davis Settlement, among which were three scalps. Perhaps it was fortunate for the girls that Gen. Whiteside had not discovered and attacked the Indians, because under such circumstances the Indians might have murdered them.

Among the troops under Gen. Whiteside was the company in which Captain Abraham Lincoln, subsequently the great president of the United States, served. Probably the girls had not yet heard of him, who, if he had known of their predicament, might have ended their captivity on that day.

During the march up the Sycamore, an old Pottawatomie Indian came into camp, tired and hungry, with a letter of safe conduct, signed by Gen. Lewis Cass. Some of the men declared the letter was a forgery, and that the Indian was a spy and should be put to death. When the soldiers threatened the poor fellow, Capt. Lincoln stepped forward and said that he would shoot any man who would assault the Indian.[21] It can be readily seen how a man of Lincoln's bravery and superior mental resources, might have freed the girls without injury to them.

---

[21]The Black Hawk War, 285.

## CHAPTER VIII.

### REWARD OFFERED.

The day after the massacre messengers carried the news in all directions to the various settlements in Illinois, southern Wisconsin, northern Indiana and western Michigan. At every settlement block-houses or stockades were built and the whites prepared to defend themselves against attacks of the Indians. At Galena the people assembled on May 28th and passed resolutions (among other things) deploring the captivity of the Hall girls and declaring their obligations to obtain the release of the captives. In Michigan along the lake shore, there was great excitement, intensified by frequent rumors that the Indians were coming.[22]

Gen. Atkinson who was then at Ottawa offered the Indians a reward of $2,000 in horses, goods or money, for the safe delivery of the girls, as it was feared that if force were used the Indians would murder the girls. In Wisconsin, Col. Dodge who had command at Blue Mounds Fort (25 miles west of Madison, Wisconsin), immediately recruited an army and made plans to get

---
[22]Michigan newspapers, 1832.

the girls. Lieutenant Edward Beouchard at Blue Mounds and Henry Gratiot of Gratiot's Grove (15 miles northeast of Galena), who were friends of the Indians with whom they had great influence, engaged in the search for the girls.

Gratiot went to Turtle Village (now Beloit, Wisconsin), where there was a tribe of Winnebagoes with whom he had been on friendly terms and who were supposed to be friends of the whites. However, the Indians took him prisoner and he almost sacrificed his life in his endeavor to obtain the release of the Hall girls. He succeeded, however, in making his message known to the Indians, and arousing among them a strong incentive to obtain the reward. While he was held as a prisoner, an Indian chief to whom Gratiot had often given presents and shown kindness, came to him and offered his services to aid in Gratiot's escape. Also Col. Gratiot was the government agent who paid the Winnebagoes their annual allowance from the United States government, which, no doubt, had some influence. The Indian took the Colonel to his tent, and late in the night silently conducted him to the river and gave him a canoe in which he paddled to safety. On his return home,

Gratiot reported that the captive girls were somewhere near the head of Rock River in southern Wisconsin. He had gleaned that much information from conversations among the Indians whose language he understood.

Not knowing that Col. Gratiot had visited Turtle Village, Gen. Anderson sent by messenger to Blue Mounds, the following letter:

"Headquarters Right Wing West. Dept., Dixon's Ferry, 27th May, 1832.

"Sir:

"In the attack of the Sac Indians on the settlements on a branch of Fox River the 22nd inst., fifteen men, women, and children, were killed, and two young women were taken prisoners. This heart-rending occurrence should not only call forth our sympathies, but urge us to relieve the survivors.

"You will therefore proceed to the Turtle Village or send someone of confidence and prevail on the head chiefs and braves of the Winnebagoes there to go over to the hostile Sacs and endeavor to ransom the prisoners. Offer the Winnebagoes a large reward to effect the object: $500 or $1000 for each.

"I expected to have heard from you before this.
Very respectfully your obt. sevt.,
H. ATKINSON,
Brig. Gen., U. S. Army."
"Henry Gratiot, Esq.,
Indian Agent."

When the dispatch reached the Mounds on May 28, Col. Gratiot who had already visited Turtle Village had not returned, and Lieutenant Beouchard who was then in command of the Fort, opened the dispatch and forwarded it to the Colonel. Also, Beouchard sent the substance of the dispatch to Col. Dodge, who was then at Fort Union, Col. Dodge's residence, near Dodgeville. Then Lieutenant Beouchard mounted his horse and rode to a Winnebago encampment which was situated northeast of Blue Mounds where Chief Wau-kon-kah was the head Indian. Beouchard requested the chief to go to White Crow, Whirling Thunder and Spotted Arm and inform them of the captivity of the Hall girls, and the reward that had been offered for their release, instructing the Indians to get the girls at any risk: by purchase, if possible; but by force, if necessary. He assured the Indians that they would receive the reward in case of success. The Indians promised to make the attempt.

May 28th, Col. Gratiot wrote a letter to Governor Porter, of Michigan, telling of the In-Indian Creek Massacre and the captivity of the Hall girls, and, among other things, said: "Compelled by our feelings and relying on the justice of our country, we did not hesitate to promise a few of my trusty Winnebagoes a reward if they would bring us those ladies unhurt. We promised them the highest reward that could be offered." Therefore, it is evident that Gratiot had offered a reward for the release of the girls before he received Gen. Anderson's dispatch.

On the day that Col. Gratiot returned from Turtle Village, he received Gen. Anderson's letter. On the same day he received further information that the Winnebagoes had success in their endeavors to ransom the unfortunate girls, and he immediately started for Blue Mounds, where he arrived on June 2nd.

## CHAPTER IX.

### THE CAPTIVE GIRLS.

In Chapter V we left the girls as prisoners at Black Hawk's Grove, Janesville, Wisconsin. Notwithstanding their night of disturbed sleep and great need for rest, the girls were awakened at daylight by the noise of the Indians around the tent.

Soon after the girls arose the squaws brought them their breakfast which consisted of dried sliced meat, coffee and porridge made of corn pounded and water, that was served in wooden bowls with wooden spoons. The little rest that the girls got through the night, revived them and gave them some appetite, so that they were able to eat part of the food, although they did not relish it.

Breakfast being finished, the Indians cleared off a piece of ground about ninety feet in circumference and erected in the center a pole about twenty-five feet high, around which they set up fifteen spears, on the points of which were placed the scalps of the murdered friends of the girls. To the horror of the girls, they recognized the scalps of their father, mother and Mrs. Pettigrew. Upon three separate spears the Indians placed three human hearts, which added greatly to the horror of the girls. Was one of the hearts their mother's?

The Indians jabbered among themselves for awhile and then the squaws painted one side of the face of each of the girls red and the other side black. Then the girls were laid with their faces downward on blankets near the center, just leaving room for the Indians to pass between them and the pole. When these preliminaries were completed, the warriors, grasping in their hands their spears, which they occasionally struck into the ground, and yelling all the while as Indians only can, danced around the girls. Every moment while this was going on, the girls expected to be thrust through with the spears; but they had become so harrassed with dread of torture, that they almost wished to have death end their troubles. However, not one of the spears touched the girls, and outside of keeping them in terror, they were in nowise injured.

After the warriors had continued their dance for about half an hour, two old squaws (one of whom was the wife of Black Hawk) led the girls away to a wigwam where they washed off the paint as well as they could by scrubbing them unmercifully. The squaws had adopted the girls, and, as the children of chiefs, they were not required to work.

The Indians having finished their dance, struck their tents, and, after a good deal of bustle and confusion, the whole camp started in a northerly direction. When they reached a point beyond the grove, it seemed to the girls that the whole earth was alive with Indians. Probably not less than 4,000 warriors, squaws, and children constituted that army.

Tired and sore from their former long ride and greatly exhausted by their constant fears, it was an extraordinary ordeal for the girls to plunge still farther into the wilderness. During traveling hours the girls were separated and each was placed in charge of two squaws. Whenever the army halted the girls were brought together, but always kept under the surveilance of the four squaws.

Their march from Black Hawk's Grove was very slow and over a broad prairie. Shortly before sundown the Indians pitched their tents at Cold Spring, about three miles southeast of Ft. Atkinson, near "Burnt Village," the camp of Little Priest.[23]

---

[23]Hist. of Jefferson Co., 327.

As soon as the tents were erected everybody partook of some food, most of the Indians without any utensils, but the girls were supplied with the usual dishes: wooden plates, bowls and spoons. At this place maple-sugar seemed to be abundant and the girls were furnished all of it that they could eat. Also, the squaws seemed to appreciate the fact that the girls were suffering from exposure, and took great pains to make their quarters as comfortable as possible.

During their long tramp through the brush, the light working dresses that the girls had on at the time that they were captured had become badly torn, and the squaws brought Rachel a red and white calico dress with ruffles around the bottom, and Sylvia, a blue calico. The Indians requested the girls to throw away their shoes and put on moccasins, against which the latter strongly protested and refused to take off their shoes. No violence to take away their shoes was used, and the girls continued to wear them. An Indian threw away Rachel's comb and she immediately went after it and kept it so that it could not be snatched away again without using force, to which the Indians did not resort.

As night set in the Indians retired and each

of the girls had to sleep between two squaws, which they were compelled to do thereafter up to the time that they were turned over to the Winnebagoes.

Day after day the Indians changed the location of their camp, probably to evade the whites if they should pursue them. From Cold Spring by circuitous routes, through the beautiful lake country around Oconomowoc, they moved northward until they reached the rolling hills near Horicon Lake where they pitched their camp not far from the rapids, and southeast of the Indian village of Big Fox.[24]

The girls had now traveled about 150 miles north from their home. It was the eighth day of their captivity, and to them the time was so long that every minute seemed almost a day; and since they last sat at dinner in the little cottage of William Davis at Indian Creek, although very vivid in their minds, seemed an age. Also, the unknown places at which they had camped being in such various directions from each other, the girls had no idea how far they had gone from Black Hawk's Grove

---

[24]V. Wis. Hist. Col., 260; Black Hawk's Autobiography, 106, 110, 160; "Waubun," 320; Hist. of Dodge Co., by Hubbell, 67.

(Janesville). Everywhere they traveled Indian camps were numerous, because as soon as spring had opened the Indians divided into small camps to make maple sugar. Were the girls to put an estimate upon the number of Indians in that unknown region, it certainly would have reached high up into the thousands.

At every camp the dance around the pole with all its hideous surroundings, accompanied by the Indian yells and war-whoops, the rattling of gourds, and waving of weapons, was repeated.

Among the tribes east of the Mississippi River it was an honor principle that their female captives should not be tortured nor their chastity violated; but if white men were taken captives they were reduced to slavery and obliged to wait upon the white women after they had been adopted by the Indians.[25] Notwithstanding this unwritten law, these dances with the scalps on the spears harrassed the girls and caused them to sob and weep bitterly.

One morning after many repetitions of the dance around the pole, the program was varied by a party of warriors coming to the lodge where the girls were in the custody of the

---

[25]1, "Handbook of American Indians," 203.

squaws, placing in their hands small red flags, and then the Indians with their captives marched around the encampment, stopping at each wigwam and waving their flags at the doors, accompanied by some recitation of a chief and the rattling of gourds, all of which was not understood by the girls and they were unable to comprehend the significance of what they were doing. As a matter of fact the performance was a religious ceremony in which the gourds took the place of bells used by several Christian denominations during their religious ceremonies.

## CHAPTER X.
### RANSOMED.

On the morning of the ninth day of their captivity, some warriors took Sylvia off about forty rods to where a number of chiefs seemed to be holding a council. One of the Indians told Sylvia that she must go with an old chief who was pointed out to her, namely, White Crow, a chief of the Winnebagoes, who was about fifty years of age, tall, slim, with a hawk nose, and as much of sinister look as a man who had only one eye could have, for one of his eyes had been put out in a brawl. He was addicted to drink, gambling, fighting, and other disreputable practices.[26] Under any circumstances Sylvia might have protested against going with him; but when he informed her that Rachel must stay behind, Sylvia declared that she would not go without her sister. White Crow, who was a fine and fluent orator, and spokesman of his band on all occasions, made a long, loud speech in which he exhibited considerable excitement, but was listened to with great interest by the other warriors. After he had finished, Chief Whirling Thunder arose, walked over to

---

[26] X. Wis. Hist. Col., 253.

where Rachel was and brought her to where the council was being held. The situation was painfully interesting to the girls, because they had some intimation that it was all about their fate. After some conversation among the chiefs they shook hands and the captives were surrendered to White Crow, who must now get the girls to Blue Mounds Fort to obtain the $2,000 reward. The Fort was about eighty miles to the southwest in a bee line. By the nearest trail through the Madison lake region, it was about ninety-three miles; and by way of Portage and thence on the Military Road to the Blue Mounds Fort, it was about one hundred and seven miles. The Sacs and Foxes were along the former route, which meant great danger, and the Military Road was the best in that country. Therefore, White Crow chose the latter route. The horses were brought, riding switches were cut and White Crow and Whirling Thunder with their captives seemed ready to go. The squaws with whom the girls had been staying were very much grieved at parting with them, tears rolling down their cheeks, and the girls who now reciprocated the affection of the squaws, preferred to stay with them rather than to go with the warriors; but the chief's stern orders had to be obeyed.

At this trying moment of the girls, a young warrior suddenly stepped up to Rachel and with a large knife cut a lock of hair from over her right ear and another from the back of her head. At the same time he muttered to White Crow, in the Indian language, something which the girls afterwards learned, was that he would have Rachel back in three or four days. His example was followed by another Indian who stepped up to Sylvia and without leave or a word of explanation, cut a lock of hair from the front of her head and placed it in his hunting-pouch. Sometime afterward a number of Indians made an attack on Kellogg's Grove colony (near Dodgeville, Wis.) and one of them who was shot by a miner named Casey had around his neck a lock of braided hair which was subsequently identified as that taken from the head of Rachel Hall.

It might not be amiss, here, to state that among some of the Indian tribes the cutting of the hair had a mystical meaning closely allied to the life of a person, and was usually attended with religious rites. The first clipping of a child's hair was retained for religious purposes.

WHERE HALL GIRLS ENTERED CANOES.

A scalp had a double meaning: it indicated an act of supernatural power that had decreed the death of the man, and it served as tangible proof of the warrior's prowess over his enemies.[27]

While the Indians were taking locks of hair from the girls, White Crow, Whirling Thunder, and a few more Indians, had mounted their horses, and with their captives on ponies, all rode off at a gallop, keeping up a rapid speed during the rest of the day and far into the night, the Indians looking back frequently.

No doubt White Crow feared that the Sacs might regret that they let the girls go, and would try to recapture them. It was about forty-seven miles to Portage, and until that place was reached the danger was great. The girls appreciated the danger; otherwise, they would have dropped off their ponies from sheer exhaustion. A ride of forty-seven miles on wabbly ponies!

Finally, they arrived on the bank of the Wisconsin River near the mouth of Duck Creek (just below Portage, Wis.) where was located a village of Chief Dekorah.[28]

---

[27]1, "Handbook of Am. Indians," 524.
[28]XIII. Wis. Hist. Co., 448; III. ib. 286; Waubun, Kinzie, 103.

## RANSOMED. 71

At this place the Indians prepared a bed upon a low scaffold, which was furnished with abundant blankets and furs, where the girls lay until daylight. The sun had not yet arisen when a party of Sac warriors, some of whom were dressed in the clothing of white men, came into camp. They wanted to talk to the girls, but Whirling Thunder told the girls not to listen to them and to keep away from them. Then a long conversation of loud angry words was kept up between the Indians for some time, when the Sacs mounted their horses and rode away.

It was ascertained later that one of the Indians who helped to capture the girls at Indian Creek was on a hunting trip when the captives were turned over to the Winnebagoes and on his return finding the prisoners gone and not having received his portion of the ransom, he started off with a number of warriors with the determination to recapture the girls or kill them. No doubt that if the Sacs had overtaken the Winnebagoes with their captives before they had reached the Winnebago camp, they would have fought for the girls, which would either have ended in the death of the girls or their being again carried off into captivity. Such was the Indian custom.[29] What an almost miraculous escape the girls had! Immediately after the Sacs left, a hastened breakfast was prepared. No doubt White Crow feared an attack if he should keep the girls at that place or if he should continue his journey along the Military Road. Whatever caused him to change his course, he arranged to take the girls down the Wisconsin River[30] and to send the horses around over the hills, on the west side of the river, to the next camping place.

Breakfast was eaten as hastily as it had been prepared and then the girls were placed in canoes and with a convoy of about one hundred Indians, were paddled off. At first the girls feared that their little barks would tip, but soon they found their canoes were in expert and safe hands and that the new manner of travel was far superior to horse-back riding. It was restful and gave them a fine opportunity for observation, which under favorable circumstances would drive an artist into ecstacy. The majestic bluffs with wooded slopes and craggy crests, lined the river for many miles, stretching off to the west around Devil's Lake. It was

---
[29]2, Handbook of American Indians, 203.
[30]Memories of Shaubena, 160.

ideal scenery and connected with many a romantic Indian tale.

The spring freshets from the melting snows and heavy rains, had swollen the river so that it spread considerably over its banks, reaching in places from the foot of one bluff to the foot of another. Down this murky water the Indians paddled their canoes, hour after hour, over a distance of about thirty miles, and landed on the west bank, where they camped for the night.

In speaking of this canoe ride the girls say: "The name of the river we never knew, neither can we tell whether we traveled up or down the stream." The name of the river was learned from Shabona. It is not strange that the girls could not tell which way the river flowed. The writer has often been on that river during freshets, and the way the water flows back and forth, dotted with eddies, would easily confuse a stranger.

Early the next morning White Crow went around to the wigwams with a gourd in each hand, and stopping at the door of each wigwam he would shake the gourd violently and talk as if he were lecturing.

Having finished this religious service, he left

the camp and did not return again until sundown. Probably, he crossed the river and went to his own village at the west end of Mendota Lake to get information concerning the ransom offered for the captives. He was a sly chief, and if he did not have considerable confidence in the success of his undertaking, instead of taking the girls across to Blue Mounds he might have them run further down the river and there hold them longer in captivity.

The thirty-first day of May had arrived and for the second night the Indians camped on the west side of the Wisconsin River. Before retiring, White Crow for the first time spoke to the girls in the English language. He inquired whether their father, mother, or any sister or brother, was alive, to which the girls replied that all had been killed on the day of their captivity. White Crow appeared sad, shook his head, and after hesitating a moment, said he would take the girls home in the morning. He asked the girls if they thought the whites would hang him if he took them to the fort, to which they replied that on the contrary the people at the fort would give him money and presents for his trouble.

The conversation with White Crow roused the

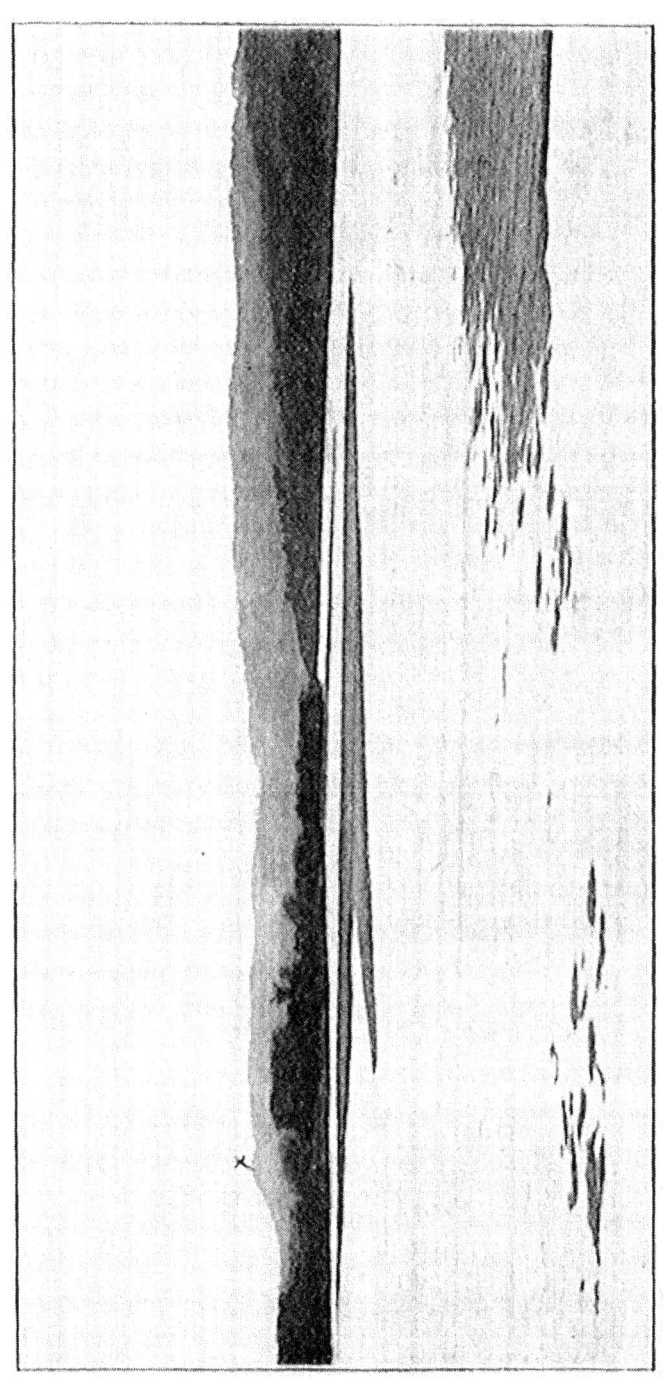

WHERE HALL GIRLS LEFT WISCONSIN RIVER.
†"BLACK HAWK'S LOOKOUT."

hopes of the girls considerably, but a lingering doubt as to the truth of his words kept revolving in their minds throughout the night.

The next morning the chiefs accompanied by about forty warriors put the girls in canoes and swam their horses across the river alongside of the canoes, landing above the mouth of Black Earth Creek. The horses were mounted in haste, but as most of the warriors had to travel on foot and were impeded by marshes and underbrush on the flat bottom, the progress was slow. The girls watched the sun with eagerness in their endeavor to tell which way they were traveling and were assured thereby that they were again going southward, although only in a circuitous course. Hour after hour passed away, the girls all the while expecting to catch sight of the fort. Finally, as the sun was sinking off over the Wisconsin River, the Indians once more camped for the night on the bank of a creek.

There were two or three Indian families camped at this place, and on seeing the girls they expressed great joy. In a short time the squaws had prepared a supper consisting of pickled pork, potatoes, coffee and bread for the girls, White Crow and Whirling Thunder, the rest of the Indians dining apart from them. The meal was the best cooked and the spread the cleanest that had been placed before the girls, and it tempted their appetite so that they made a very fair meal, after which they felt sleepy and were glad when they could lie down to rest. In a short time most of the Indians had retired, excepting White Crow, who seated himself close to the girls, where he smoked a pipe all night. This was the first time that a warrior had kept guard over them, and the inference of the girls was that the old chief feared an attack of the Sacs who had visited their camp at Portage. The girls thought that perhaps the Indian chief who had been rebuffed at that place might have gone after recruits, and that at any moment the Indians might swoop down upon them. Now, when they were almost within grasp of their freedom, it racked the minds of the girls to think that there was a possibility of being slaughtered or again carried into captivity. In this condition of mind the girls passed the night.

The camp was astir at sunrise and for the last time White Crow went around performing his religious service by rattling his gourds and addressing the Indians. After breakfast the girls were again mounted on their ponies and all moved forward over higher ground, and before ten o'clock they had reached the Military Road from Fort Winnebago, by way of Blue Mounds, to Prairie du Chien. The sight of the wagon tracks was the first sign of civilization that the girls had observed since their captivity and increased their confidence in the probability of their early release. Also, the road was much better than any they had traveled since their capture. It led through groves and oak openings, along the high ridge that is unbroken to the Mississippi River. Inspirations of hope were necessary to revive the girls' spirits and enable them to complete the remainder of their long journey, as they were exhausted to the verge of collapse. Hope is a great stimulant, and it was on this that the girls were now subsisting.

"Auspicious Hope! in thy sweet garden grow
Wreaths for each toil, a charm for every woe."

About two o'clock in the afternoon the Indians halted for lunch and to let their horses feed. The principal food was duck eggs, nearly hatched, that the Indians ate with relish, but which the girls rejected with disgust. After lunch they had not traveled far until they caught sight of Blue Mounds Fort in the distance. White Crow took a white handkerchief that Rachel had tied on her head, which he fastened on a pole for a flag of truce, and rode in advance of the Indians and their captives. In a short time Lieutenant Edward Beouchard, who was commander at the fort, met them and addressed the Indians in their own language. The warriors now formed a circle into which Beouchard rode and he and the Indians talked at considerable length. According to Beouchard's subsequent statement the Indians were unwilling to give up the girls until they were assured by Col. Gratiot that the $2,000 reward would be paid. Beouchard having assured the girls that they would be well treated by the Indians until his return, went back to the fort and soon returned with Col. Henry Gratiot, the Indian agent, and a company of soldiers in which Edward and Reason Hall, uncles of the captives, were serving as privates.

Col. Gratiot assured the Indians that the reward for the rescue of the girls would be paid. Also, he invited the Indians to be his guests at the fort, and that he would prepare a big feast for them. The Indians being very hungry the feast appealed very strongly to them. Finally, the chiefs agreed to place the girls in the custody of Col. Gratiot until the reward would be paid, the Indians retaining the right to the return of the captives if the government failed to pay.

The calico dresses which the girls had received from the Indians, had become torn by riding through brake, briars and brush, and with their soiled faces and disheveled hair, made them objects of pity.[31] In a sense, the girls bearing their crosses, had followed their Master up Calvary to its summit, where He granted their prayer by setting them free.

[31] 3, Smith's Hist. of Wis., 214, 225.

## CHAPTER XI.
### ROYALLY WELCOMED.

Following close behind the soldiers that went out with Col. Gratiot to meet the Indians with the girls, were the ladies of the Fort, including the wives of the commanding officers, and although the Indians had delivered the girls into the custody of Col. Gratiot, the ladies immediately took charge of them, and after kissing and hugging them affectionately, conducted them to the Fort, where the girls were furnished with new clothes and the best meal that the place could produce. After dining the girls became sleepy and retired to rest, feeling perfectly secure.

> "Sleep! to the homeless thou are home;
> The friendless find in thee a friend;
> And well is, wheresoe'er he roam,
> Who meets thee at his journey's end."

A messenger who had been dispatched for Col. Dodge, met him on his way to the Mounds in company with Capt. Bion Gratiot, a brother of Col. Henry Gratiot. On his arrival Col. Dodge immediately assumed general command of the place. He invited the Indian chiefs, White Crow, Whirling Thunder and Spotted

Arm, into the Fort, and fed them sumptuously. Ebenezer Brigham who lived at the east end of the Mounds contributed a big fat steer for the feast. After the feast, lodgings for the Indians were prepared, beds for the chiefs having been provided in one of the cottages. Having everything comfortably arranged, the Colonel retired and was soon fast asleep.

About an hour after Col. Dodge had gone to bed, Capt. Gratiot came rushing to his cabin in an excited manner, calling to him to rouse up and prepare for action immediately. He informed the Colonel that the Indian chiefs whom the Colonel had placed in the cottage, had gone out to some brush near by and apparently were inciting the Indians to make an attack upon the Fort. White Crow had come to the Captain and after telling him that the whites were a softshelled breed and no good to fight (referring to Stillman's defeat), he closed by advising the Captain to tell his brother, Col. Gratiot, the Indians' friend, to go home and not stay at the fort. Also, Capt. Gratiot had observed the men whetting their knives, tomahawks and spears, and it was learned that two of the warriors had been sent to the Winnebago camp early in the evening, probably to obtain more Indians to attack the Fort.

Col. Dodge, after listening attentively to the story of Capt. Gratiot, replied: "Do not be alarmed, sir; I will see that no harm befalls you."

Col. Dodge then called the officer of the guard and an interpreter and with six other men went out to where the Indians were and took into custody White Crow and five of the other principal chiefs, and marched them into a cabin inside the palisade to secure obedience to his command. Then after directing the proper officer to place a strong guard around the cabin and double the guard around the whole encampment, the Colonel lay down with the Indians. To carry out the Colonel's orders took all the men at the Fort, so that virtually the whole force was under arms during the night.[32] Once more the girls' lives were in jeopardy.

The night passed without another incident and when the sun arose over the great plains to the east, the girls were up and relished a good breakfast with their friends that awaited them.

---
[32] X. Wis. Hist. Col., 186.

Col. Dodge was out before the girls and he told the Indians that they must all go to Morrison's Grove, a place where the road to Galena branches off the Military Road to Prairie du Chien, about fifteen miles west of Blue Mounds. The Indians—White Crow particularly—protested against going, stating that their feet were sore from their long march in bringing the Hall girls to the Mounds, and that they had shown such great magnanimity in risking their lives to ransom the prisoners that they should receive their reward and be allowed to return home. Col. Dodge frankly told them that he believed that they were in sympathy with Black Hawk and that he should be obliged to treat them as suspects. In vain did White Crow use his eloquence in protesting his friendship for the whites, and after all was in readiness the Indians and soldiers accompanied by the Hall girls started on their march to Morrison's Grove, where they arrived before noon. Here George Medary kept a hotel in a large house built by the Morrison brothers of hewn logs, adjoining a cultivated field, one of the first in the state.[33]

The ladies looked after the comfort of the

---

[33]XIII. Wis. Hist. Col., 341; "Waubun," 111.

girls, whom they welcomed with much exhibition of joy and affection, and Col. Dodge, after having the Indians well fed, ordered the chiefs to line them up until he could talk to them.

First Col. Dodge explained the alarming situation surrounding the white settlers, and the information that he had that the Winnebagoes were hesitating to join Black Hawk, and warned them of their destruction if they should take part in the war against the whites. Next Col. Gratiot spoke to the Indians in their own tongue, in a kindly manner, and after he had finished White Crow made the following speech: "Fathers, when you sent a request to me to go and to ransom those two white women, we called on all of our people who were around us and they gave all of their wampum, trinkets and corn, and we the chiefs gave ten horses. The Little Priest, I, and two others, went to the Sauks to buy the prisoners. We soon succeeded in buying one, but for a time could not succeed in buying the other. After we had bought one, we demanded the other. They said, 'No, we will not give her up. We have lost too much blood. We will keep her.'

"We told them: 'If you don't give her up, we will raise the tomahawk and take her.' I had a horse which you, father (Gratiot), gave me. It was the last horse that I had. I told them that I would give them that horse to obtain the prisoner. At sundown they gave me the girls and I gave them the horse. The Little Priest took one of the girls and I took the other and put them on horses. A Sauk came, as we were about to start, and attempted to cut off the hair of one of the girls. I caught his hand and prevented him, but allowed him afterwards to cut a small lock. These white sisters were very much affected and my young daughter cried to see these white sisters so distressed. Our women bought clothes from the Sauks and gave them. These sisters will tell you that we made them sleep together, and the daughter of the Little Priest slept on one side of them and my daughter on the other side. We were mortified that we could not use them better. Our blankets are worn out and we could do no better. I tried to please and comfort them, but they were not accustomed to our mode of living and could not eat.

"Here are our two sisters, we bring them here to take their hands and give them into your hands. We have saved their lives, for the Sauks intended to kill them.

"And now, fathers, all that we have to ask of you is that you will not put us or our children in the same situation that these white sisters were. We have brought them to you to prove to you that we are the friends of the Americans."[34]

After listening to White Crow, Col. Dodge informed him that he would hold as hostages for the good conduct of the Winnebago Indians, their chiefs Spotted Arm, Whirling Thunder and Little Priest, to which the wiley chief made little objection, as he was trying to obtain as much goods as possible in final settlement of the reward, which was paid mostly in trinkets, blankets and horses.

Having been well fed and supplied with shawls and blankets of brilliant colors, child-like, the Indians were now anxious to go home.

White Crow, with a showing of much regret, bade good-bye to Sylvia and Rachel Hall. He went over the incidents of their rescue, and, to prove his friendship for the girls, offered to give each of them a Sac squaw as a servant for life. The girls thanked him, but said that they did not want any human being to be taken away from her people as they had been from theirs.

---

[34]Report of Col. Gratiot in U. S. files.

The girls then bade adieu to all the Indians, towards whom their hearts had changed, and for whom they now felt considerable friendship. The eloquence of White Crow made an impression on the young women, as he spoke in a sympathetic tone unexpected kind words that touched their hearts.

After resting at Morrison's during the afternoon and night, early the next morning the soldiers with their Indian hostages and the girls, proceeded along the Galena road to Fort Defiance, which was located five miles southeast of Mineral Point. Here again the girls were well cared for by the wives of the officers, and the most sumptuous meal that could be prepared was set before them, and their short stay made as pleasant as possible.[35]

After dinner, with the convoy of soldiers and the Indian hostages, the girls again moved on to Gratiot's Grove, about a mile south of Shullsburg, and fourteen miles northeast of Galena. At this place there was a village of twenty families, with a hotel and a garrison of United States soldiers.[36] The leading lady of the place was Capt. Gratiot's wife, a French woman of excellent education, whose mother had been

---
[35] X. Wis. Hist., Col., 340.

lady-in-waiting to Queen Marie Antoinette. Mrs. Gratiot, who was noted for her hospitality, took charge of the girls and entertained them lavishly at her home.[37]

Gratiot's Grove, which became renowned as the most beautiful spot in the northwest, is described by Mrs. Gratiot as follows: "Never in my wanderings had I beheld a prettier place; the beautiful rolling hills extending to Blue Mounds, a distance of thirty miles, the magnificent grove, as yet untouched by the falling axe, formed the graceful frame for the lovely landscape."[38] Theodore Rudolph, a Swiss traveler who was at Gratiot's Grove in the spring of 1832, describing the place says: "The vast prairie, as far as the eye could reach, was clothed with a carpet of richest green, interspersed with gorgeous wild flowers, of brilliant hues of red, blue, and yellow, in fact every color of the rainbow—reminding one of the garden of Eden, as our youthful fancies never failed to paint it for us."[39]

[36] X. Wis. Hist. Col., 256.
[37] X. Wis. Hist. Col., 186, 246.
[38] X. Wis. Hist. Col., 286.
[39] XV. Wis. Hist. Col., 345.

## CHAPTER XII.

### HOMEWARD BOUND.

"Oh! sweet is the longed-for haven of rest!
And dear are the loved ones we oft have caressed!
And fair are the home scenes that gladden the
   view—
The far-wooded hills stretching up to the blue,
The lake's limpid splendor, the circling shore,
The fell and the forest, the mead and the moor,
   Are clustered with mem'ries and, though we may
   roam,
Their charm ever guides us and whispers of home!"
—Anna C. Scanlan.

The thought of returning to their home filled the girls' hearts with such joy as was possible under their circumstances. When they arose on the morning of their departure from Gratiot's Grove, everything was inspiring. Never before had the birds sung more sweetly nor had the flowers looked more beautiful. The whole village was astir early, and probably there was not one of the inhabitants who failed to appear to bid the girls good-bye.

Capt. Gratiot's wife made the girls some nice presents and had so endeared herself to them that although they had known her but a very short time, they left her with tears, and in tears.

Finally, all being ready, with a convoy of soldiers the girls continued their journey to White

## HOMEWARD BOUND.

Oak Springs (10 miles northeast of Galena), near which they formerly lived and where they had many friends. It was then a mining village of considerable size, but not so charming as Gratiot's Grove. There was a fort with soldiers at the place, and all was in readiness to receive the girls. As some of their relatives lived near the place, going there seemed to them like going home.

One of the first surprises that the girls had, was to meet their brother John who they thought had been murdered at Indian Creek. He had been mustered into the militia and was stationed at Galena, but was granted indefinite absence to go to meet his sisters and accompany them home.

At White Oak Springs they received a letter from their former pastor, Rev. R. Horn, who had a mission on the Illinois River where Robert Scott, an uncle of the girls, lived. The letter was full of kindness and invited the girls to come to the Horn residence and make it their home. From that time on, all arrangements were made to that end.

On the night of June sixteenth, great excitement was caused by a messenger riding into the town and announcing that the battle of the

Peckatonica (18 miles northeast) had been fought, that all the Indians that participated in it had been killed, and that many of the whites had fallen. The shocking particulars, which were loathing to the girls, were told and retold. They had seen human blood spilled and they knew what such a sight meant, so it simply renewed their horror.

The girls remained at White Oak Springs two weeks, during which their lady friends made considerable clothing for them so that they had a well-supplied wardrobe, considering the time and the border country. The men were not backward in the good work and presents of goods were given by the store-keepers and a small purse raised to help to smooth their way.

Also, old acquaintances were renewed and new friendships were formed from which it was hard to break away when it came time to leave. From gruff old miners up to the army officer in his shoulder-straps, the village folk gathered around the young ladies to wish them God-speed.

The girls shook hands with everybody and thanked them, individually and collectively, for their great kindness. In the last written statement signed by Rachel Hall Munson and Sylvia

Hall Horn, they say: "We are very sorry we cannot recollect the names of those kind friends, that they might appear upon record as a testimony of their kindness to us in our destitute condition. May the blessings of our Father in heaven, rest upon them all!"

From White Oak Springs the girls went on to Galena, where they stopped with an old acquaintance named Bell and were supplied with rations by the United States' army officers who considered the girls their guests.

They had not been there many days before the steamboat "Winnebago" called for a load of lead to take to St. Louis. The girls with their brother John and their uncle Edward Hall took passage down the Mississippi to St. Louis where they arrived June 30, and were received by Gov. Clark who took them to his home and entertained them as his guests.[40]

Unfortunately, at that time the cholera was in the city and meetings of people, public demonstrations, and entertainments, were restricted. While the girls did not feel like attending entertainments or going in society, the people of St. Louis were anxious to entertain them.

[40] Letter of Governor Clark to Secretary of War, June 30, 1832; "Life of A. S. Johnston," Johnston, 23.

A purse of $470.00 was collected, and, at the request of the girls, was put into the hands of Mr. Horn for investment. Other small sums of money were given to the girls to pay their incidental expenses, and articles for their comfort were presented to them.

The girls were anxious to go home, and in company with their brother John and Uncle Edward they boarded the steamer "Carolina" for Beardstown, Ill., from where they were taken to the home of their uncle Robert Scott, close to Mr. Horn's. Here they remained until Fall, when they went to the home of their brother John who had recently married and settled on a homestead in Bureau County, about twenty miles west of the Davis Settlement.

## CHAPTER XIII.
### ROMANCE AND HISTORY.

At a little country store down in Indiana where the settlers usually gathered to read the weekly newspaper, William Munson, a young man who was born in New York, first heard of the Hall girls and their wonderful adventure. He was in the west seeking his fortune, and, being an admirer of the brave and full of youthful fire, he remarked to the people that he would some day marry one of those girls. His nearest friends did not take him seriously, and the matter as a passing joke was soon forgotten. However, with him it became a fixed idea, and in the spring of 1833 he went to Illinois and took up a land claim in the neighborhood where John W. Hall lived.

Every good woman is not satisfied until she has a home of her own. This natural longing was particularly strong in the minds of the Hall girls, whose home had been destroyed.

There is no record of how William Munson first met Rachel Hall, but our information shows that their courtship was short; for in March, 1833, they were united in marriage, and shortly afterwards they settled down on the land claim entered by her father, about a mile and a half

WILLIAM MUNSON.

east of the scene of the massacre. They were thrifty and got along splendidly, becoming one of the foremost families of La Salle County. Besides the rich abundance of worldly goods, they were blessed with a large family of whom four died in their infancy. As there was no cemetery, the little ones were buried in the garden. Of the other children who grew up to manhood and womanhood, several became very prominent and their generations became numerous. Their four daughters were married as

MRS. RACHEL HALL MUNSON, AGED 42, AND YOUNGEST SON ELLIOT.

follows: Irma, to Dr. George Vance, who moved to California; A. Miranda, to Samuel Dunavan, who settled on a farm just north of the Munson homestead, where she still lives; Fidelia, to George Shaver, and Phoebe B., to John F. Reed, of Ottawa. Mr. Reed's daughter Fannie married James H. Eckles who was United States Treasurer under Cleveland. Mrs. Eckles' daughter Winnie is married to Judge Kenesaw Mountain Landis, of Chicago. William Munson, Jr., married Delia Shaver, and the other surviving sons, Louis and Elliot, never married.

Edward Vance, a grand-son of Mrs. Munson, is a well-known lawyer in South Dakota, and Douglas Dunavan is a prominent lawyer at Ottawa, Illinois. We shall not attempt to give sketches of the various descendents of Mrs. Munson, as it would expand too much the limits of this volume.

The shock of the massacre and consequent captivity impaired the splendid constitution of Mrs. Munson, who thereafter suffered from nervousness; but through the earlier part of her life, she manifested unusual vigor. As Mrs. Munson passed middle life she failed rapidly, and on May 1, 1870, she closed her earthly career and was laid to rest in the garden beside her infant children who had gone before her, and when Mr. Munson died he was interred beside his faithful wife. Their graves are about one and one-half miles east of Shabona Park, on the original Hall homestead.

BURIAL PLACE OF RACHEL AND HUSBAND.

Incidentally, we noted the fact that for a short spell the Hall girls made their home at the residence of Rev. Robert Horn. He had a young son, William S., who was studying for the ministry, and as both belonged to the same church (M. E. Episcopal) and were born in Kentucky, we cannot say that the unexpected happened. He was one year younger than Sylvia. The love story of these young people would gratify any novel writer. When Sylvia left with her sister to make her home with her brother John, she and Mr. Horn looked upon each other with great affection. The marriage of Rachel emphasized the yearnings of Sylvia for her own home, and May 5, 1833, she was married to Mr. Horn and settled in Cass County, Illinois. There were born to Mr. and Mrs. Horn. eleven children. Mr. Horn's vocation called him from one place to another. Having served in the ministry in Illinois, he first went to Missouri, thence to Peru, Nebraska, next to a parish near Lincoln, and finally settled down at Auburn, Nemaha County, Nebraska, where he died May 8, 1888, leaving him surviving, his widow, Mrs. Sylvia Hall Horn, and several children and grand-children.

Mr. Horn became an elder of the M. E. Episcopal church, and held several high church offices. Elder Horn was noted for his intense religious zeal, and, figuratively speaking, he died in the harness of exhaustion and old age. He was buried in Mt. Vernon Cemetery, Peru, Nebraska.

After the death of Elder Horn, Mrs. Sylvia Hall Horn made her home with her son, Thomas S. Horn, in Auburn, Nebraska, where she died January 11, 1899, aged 85 years, 10 months and

MRS SYLVIA HALL HORN AND ELDER HORN.

16 days. Mrs. Horn was buried beside her husband with whom she had happily lived for 55 years. She left surviving her a host of descendants.

In the fall of 1867, John W. Hall, Mrs. Munson, and her husband, made a visit to Elder Horn's, Auburn, Nebraska, during which Mr. Hall and his sisters narrated the incidents of the massacre and captivity, which were reduced to writing by the Elder and published. The manuscripts are now in the custody of Mrs. Eckels of Chicago. In his statement Mr. Hall says: "After thirty-five years of toil have pased over my head since the memorable occasion, my memory is in some things rather dim." Mrs. Munson and Mrs. Horn close their recital as follows: "Thus we have given the circumstances of our captivity and the rescue as nearly as we can recollect at this date, September 7, 1867." The former published statements of the ladies substantially agree with this last one. All their statements and public interviews have been freely used and completely worked into this narrative.[41]

In 1833 the state of Illinois donated to Mrs.

---

"3 Smith's "History of Wisconsin" (1854), 187; "The Black Hawk War" (Stevens), 150.

THREE GENERATIONS OF RACHEL.

1, Mrs. Dunavan (daughter); 3, Mrs. Hum and 4 Mrs. Watts (grand-daughters); 5, Howard and 6 Gladys Hum and 7 Baby Watts (great-grandchildren); 2, Samuel Dunavan (son-in-law); and 8, Mrs. Rogers (neighbor).

Munson and Mrs. Horn, 160 acres of land that the United States had given to the state towards the construction of the canal between Chicago and Ottawa. At that time the land was not valuable, and netted but a small sum to the ladies. Now that land is within the city of Joliet and is worth considerable money.

It has been asserted—and published in books, that Congress voted gifts of money to the girls; but in answer to an inquiry made at the United States Treasury, the author was informed that no such appropriation has ever been made, and Mrs. Dunavan says that she never knew of her mother's receiving any money from the government.

In 1837 Mr. Munson erected a very handsome monument on the spot where his wife's parents and the others who died with them were buried. It is a graceful shaft.

In 1905, through the efforts of friends of the persons who were massacred at Indian Creek on May 21st, 1832, the Illinois legislature appropriated the sum of five thousand dollars to place a monument at the grave where the victims were buried.[42] On August 29, 1906, the

---

[42]Laws of Illinois, 1905, p. 42.

new monument was dedicated with much ceremony, music and orations. Among the speakers were the venerable Hon. John W. Henderson and his brother, Gen. T. J. Henderson, who were boys at the time that the massacre occurred, the former being one of the persons who were planting corn south of the Davis cottage on that day, and who with John W. Hall escaped to Ottawa.

A full account of the dedication will be found in the newspapers and in the records of the Illinois Historical Society.[43]

[43]"Ottawa Journal," August 30, 1906; "Bureau County Republican," August 30, 1906; XII., "Transactions of the Illinois State Historical Society," p. 339.

## CHAPTER XIV.

### SHABONA.*

The story of the Hall girls' adventures would not be properly finished without some further mention of Chief Shabona. Probably no other Indian in the West knew more white people, individually, than he knew; also, he was known at sight to more white people than was any other chief of his time. His name was so familiar among the whites, that its mere mention was a safe passport to any home of the settlers.

---

*This chief's name is spelled in many different ways, to-wit: "Sha-bom-ri," in Smith's History of Wisconsin; "Shah-bee-nay," by Mrs. Kinzie in Wau-Bun; "Shaubena," by Matson; "Shau-be-nee," by Kingston; "Chab-on-eh," "Shab-eh-ney," "Shabonee," and "Shaubena," in the Appleton's Encyclopedia of American Biographies, and on his tombstone his name is spelled "Shabona". In Illinois, places named after him are spelled Shabbona and Shabonier, the latter being the French spelling. As Mr. Smith, Mrs. Kinzie, Mr. Matson, and Mr. Kingston, knew Shabona well, the weight of evidence seems to be in favor of spelling his name Shaubena, which is in accordance with the spelling of Indian words. The second b is not heard in the usual pronounciation of "Shabbona" (Shab'-eh-ney), and it causes strangers to mispronounce the name. Even the word "Sac", is usually pronounced Sauk, and is generally spelled Sauk. Very many Indian names have the diphthong au as shown by names of rivers and places. Consequently, it would seem that the first syllable should be spelled S-h-a-u-b.

[106]

Shabona was well aware of that fact and he always introduced himself as "Mr. Shabona." Baldwin says that Shabona was born in Canada; but Matson asserts that he was born on the Kankakee in Will County, Illinois; and the "Handbook of American Indians" gives Maumee River, Illinois, as his birthplace. This contention of many countries as the place of Shabona's birth, proves the greatness of the man. Argos, Rhodes, Smyrna, Chios, Colophon, and several other cities, claim to be the birthplace of Homer; and Scotland, England, Wales, and Britany, of St. Patrick. Authors agree that Shabona was born in 1775 and dwelt at Shabona's Grove for fifty years. He was a grandnephew of Pontiac and his father who was an Ottawa chief, fought under Pontiac. Shabona was six feet tall, erect, and weighed over two hundred pounds.

During the wars of 1812, 1827 and 1832, Shabona rendered great services to the white people by saving the lives of many of them who were taken captives by the Indians, and by protecting the home of John Kinzie and his friends during the Chicago massacre. However, with his tribe he joined in the border war against the whites and fought beside Tecumseh when he fell at the battle of the Thames. That was the last time that Shabona raised a hand against the white people.

When Col. Richard M. Johnson, who commanded the American army at the Thames became vice-president of the United States, Shabona made a visit to him at Washington. The vice-president gave Shabona a heavy gold ring, which he wore until his death and at his request it was buried with him.

On account of Shabona's great services to the white people, the state of Illinois gave him two and one-half sections of land at the site of his Paw-Paw Village. In 1837 the last of Shabona's tribe having been moved to a Kansas reservation, he followed them with his family consisting of twenty-seven persons, including his son Pypagee and nephew Pyps who were soon thereafter slain by the Sacs for the parts that they played in notifying the whites to flee to Ottawa, before the massacre at Indian Creek. Shabona was warned that the Sacs were scheming to assassinate him, because of his efforts to save the whites, and in 1855 he returned to Illinois.

Before Shabona left Illinois for Kansas, he placed his lands in the hands of an agent named

Norton to collect the rents, pay the taxes and to look after them generally. Unconscionable settlers squatted on Shabona's lands and filed in the government land office, affidavits that Shabona had abandoned the lands, and on that proof and some technicalities the lands were again sold as public lands, and on Shabona's return he found his domain in the possession of the squatters who claimed to be the owners. Shabona could not help feeling that he had been cheated by the whites, after all he had done for them, and the old man sat on a log near where his village had formerly stood and wept bitterly.

> "And man, whose heaven-erected face
> The smiles of love adorn,
> Man's inhumanity to man
> Makes countless thousands mourn!"

Shortly after his return, as Shabona was cutting a few poles to erect a tent on the margin of the grove that bore his name, a settler attacked him and forcibly drove him off the land, and shamefully abused the old man. Then for some time homeless, he wandered about from place to place, the few remaining whites whom he had befriended, always giving him a warm welcome. The old warrior's plight aroused the dormant gratitude of a few whites who raised a fund with which they bought for him at Seneca, on Mazon Creek, near the Illinois River, twenty acres of land which they cultivated and erected a dwelling-house thereon. Because of his natural desire to live out-doors, Shabona lived in a tent nearby and used the cottage for storage purposes. Through the efforts of his friends, the government granted him a pension of two hundred dollars a year, on which he subsisted until he died in 1859, at the age of eighty-four years, and was buried in Evergreen Cemetery, at Morris, Illinois.[44]

When Shabona was dying, he said: "I want no monument erected to my memory; my life has been mark enough for me." However, his friends erected at his grave a granite boulder five feet long by three feet high, which bears only this simple inscription: "Shabona, 1775-1859."[45]

[44]7, Wis. Hist. Col., 415-421; History of La Salle County, Balwin, 110.
[45]"Evergreen Cemetery" (printed pamphlet), p. 4.

## CHAPTER XV.
### CO-MEE AND TO-QUA-MEE.

Some of our readers may ask, Was anyone prosecuted for the massacre at Indian Creek? Oh, yes! Co-mee and To-qua-mee who had tried to buy Rachel and Sylvia Hall from their father, as related in Chapter III., were, in the spring of 1833, at Ottawa, Illinois, indicted by a grand jury, and a warrant issued and placed in the hands of Sheriff George E. Walker who had been an Indian trader and spoke the Pottawatomie language, to make the arrests. The Indians had gone to Iowa with Black Hawk and had become members of his tribe.

Alone, Sheriff Walker went to the Sac reservation and placed the Indians under arrest. The two Indians made no resistance, but unshackled accompanied the sheriff to Ottawa. They were allowed to go on a bond signed by themselves, Shabona, and several other Indians, upon their promises upon their honor to return for trial.

When the time for the trial arrived the Indians were on hand, although they had told their friends that they expected to be executed. Many of the friends of the people who had been massacred, armed and threatening to shoot the prisoners, if they should be liberated, attended the trial. There was no jail in Ottawa at the time, so the trial was held under a great tree on the bank of the Illinois. All through the trial the sheriff with a posse of armed men, guarded the Indians.

Mrs. Munson and Mrs. Horn, the principal witnesses, could not positively identify either of the Indians, and as the Indians had voluntarily stood their trial when they might have escaped, the jury acquitted them. When the trial was over the Indians' friends gave them a banquet at Buffalo Rock (six miles down the Illinois), to which the sheriff and several other prominent men of the time were invited. A fat deer and choice game were parts of the menu, and a great red-white pow-wow was a part of the celebration.

It is said that subsequently when To-qua-mee and Co-mee were drinking with their friends, they admitted that they were present at the massacre, and that they took part in it only because they were angered at Davis for building the dam across Indian Creek. Also, they stated that it was through their influence that the lives of the Hall girls were spared, which was an express condition upon which they insisted before they would take part in the massacre. However, Black Hawk in his autobiography states that it was the Sac Indians who saved the lives of the girls; and White Crow in his speech at Morrison's, said that the Sacs intended to kill the girls and that the Winnebagoes saved their lives.[46]

[46]XI. Transactions of Illinois Historical Society, 1906, p. 313; Memories of Shabona, 165-168; Black Hawk's Autobiography, 111; Ante, p. 83.

# INDEX

## A.
| | PAGE |
|---|---|
| Adoption of Captives by chiefs | 61 |
| Agriculture and civilization | 25 |
| Atkinson, Gen. at Ottawa | 51 |
| letter to Col. Gratiot | 56 |
| offers reward | 54 |
| Auburn, where Elder Horn died | 100 |

## B.
Battle of "Stillman's Run" .............. 20
The Pecatonica........ 92
Beloit, Turtle village... 55
Beouchard, Lieut. Edward .............. 55
meeting captives...... 79
Big Fox, camp near..... 63
Black Earth Creek, camp on ................... 76
Black Hawk War....... 17
Black Hawk, born at Rock Island......... 18
council of............. 18
fought with English, 1812 ................ 18
grief of............... 19
love of country........ 18
ordered to move to Iowa ............... 18
return to Illinois..... 18
speech of ............ 18
second council of..... 20
Black Hawk's Grove, arrival at ............. 45
Black Hawk "Lookout", camp near ......... 75
Black Hawk, picture of as a warrior......... 17
picture of as civilian.. 21
Black Hawk's village... 26
Blacksmith, important settler .............. 25

## C.
Blockhouses, building of 54
Brigham, Ebenezer, Indian feast .......... 82
Buckwheat as first crop. 25
Buffalo, herds of........ 12
"Burnt City", near Ft. Atkinson, Wis. ..... 61

Camp on Wisconsin river .............. 74
Black Hawk's Grove 45, 59
Black Hawk's "Lookout", camp near.... 75
Cold Spring .......... 61
Horicon Lake ........ 63
Portage, camp near... 70
Canada, Indian voyages to .................... 26
Canoes, where girls entered ............... 68
Captives, Indians kill when attacked ...... 71
Captivity of Hall girls.. 38
"Carolina", St. Louis to Beardstown ......... 94
Chickens, prairie ....... 12
Chippewas, Indians..... 16
Cholera at St. Louis.... 93
Civilization, marriage and agriculture..... 25
Clark, Gov., of Missouri. 93
Clothes, Indians furnish Hall girls .......... 62
Cold Spring, camping at 61
Comb, Rachel's thrown away ............... 62
Co-mee, tried to buy wife ................ 23
arrest of for murder.. 111
acquittal ............ 112
alleged confession of murder ............ 113
Country, description of. 9

[114]

# INDEX 115

### D.
| | PAGE |
|---|---|
| Dam across Indian Creek | 29 |
| Indians object to | 29 |
| Indian tears outlet through | 29 |
| Dancing of Indians 41, 59, | 64 |
| Davis City, dream of | 28 |
| Davis, Jefferson | 9 |
| Davis Settlement | 23 |
| Davis, Alex., escape of | 32 |
| Davis, William, sketch of | 25 |
| children of murdered. | 35 |
| murdered by Indians | 35 |
| powerful and brave | 28 |
| whipped Indian with stick | 29 |
| Davis, Wm., Jr., escape of | 35 |
| Dedication of State Monument | 105 |
| Deer, herds of | 12 |
| Description of country | 9 |
| Dixon, center of trails | 13 |
| Dodge, Col., raises troops | 54 |
| address to Indians | 85 |
| command at Blue Mounds | 81 |
| takes hostages | 87 |
| Drunkenness in Militia | 52 |
| "Dry Year", the | 31 |
| Dunavan, Mrs. A. Miranda | 6, 97, 103 |
| information given by | 6 |
| Dunavan, Samuel, married Miss Munson | 97 |
| picture of | 103 |

### E.
| | |
|---|---|
| Eckles, Hon. James H., U. S. Treasurer | 98 |
| Eckles, Winnie, married to Judge Landis | 98 |
| English government pensioned Sacs | 26 |
| Evidence, best | 6 |

### F.
| | |
|---|---|
| Family history, Munson | 6, 95 |
| Family history, Horn. | 6, 100 |
| Fire, a prairie | 11 |
| Flag of Truce | 20, 79 |
| Flowers, many beautiful | 12, 27 |
| great growth of | 31 |
| Forests, trees of | 10 |
| Fort Defiance, rest at | 78 |
| Fort Winnebago, Portage | 78 |
| Fox Indians | 13 |
| Fox river, description of | 9 |

### G.
| | |
|---|---|
| Galena, meeting of people | 54 |
| Game, abundance of | 12 |
| Geology of country | 10 |
| George, Henry, at work on dam | 32 |
| shot by Indians | 36 |
| Gratiot, Capt. Bion, and Indians | 81 |
| wife of, cultured | 89, 90 |
| Gratiot, Col. Henry, Indians' friend | 55 |
| address to Indians | 84 |
| Gratiot's Grove, description of | 89 |

### H.
| | |
|---|---|
| Hair, ceremony of clipping | 68, 70 |
| cutting locks from captives | 68 |
| scalp, double meaning of | 70 |
| Hall girls, as captives | 41-47, 59-65 |
| adopted by chiefs | 61 |
| and neighbors' horses. | 39 |
| at Black Earth Creek | 76, 77 |
| at Black Hawk s Grove | 45 |
| at Blue Mounds | 79-83 |
| at Cold Spring | 61 |
| at Fort Defiance | 88 |
| at Galena | 93 |
| at Gratiot's Grove | 88-90 |
| at Horicon, Lake | 66-67 |
| at Kishwaukee river. | 42-44 |
| at Morrison's | 84-88 |
| at Portage | 70 |
| at St. Louis | 93 |
| at White Oak Springs | 90-92 |
| description of | 7, 8 |
| dresses given by squaws | 62 |

# 116 INDEX

food of captives...... 43, 46, 62, 72, 76, 78
guests of Gov. Clark.. 93
Indians wanted as wives ............... 23
kept apart in traveling 61
letter from Rev. Horn. 91
painted by squaws.... 60
popular appellation of. 6
prayers of ............ 39
presents to .... 92, 102, 104
purse collected for.... 94
Rachel exhausted... 42, 98
religious offerings .... 46
sleeping between squaws ............. 46
tiresome traveling.42, 70, 78
weeping of ......... 39, 90
wept parting squaws.. 79
Hall, Edward, in militia 79
Hall, Elizabeth, killed by Indians ....... 23, 35
Hall, Greenbury, escape of ................ 32, 36
Hall, John W., escape of ................ 35, 36
buries massacred whites ............... 49
meets sisters ......... 91
recruits squadron .... 48
searches for sisters.. 49, 50
statement of ......... 102
visits sisters in Nebraska ............... 102
Hall, Reason, in Militia. 79
Hall, Rachel, one of the "Hall girls", ages of 23, 98
death of ............. 98
exhausted .......... 42, 98
family of ........... 96, 98
marriage of .......... 95
picture of ........... 97
state land gift........ 102
tomb of ............. 99
wading Kishwaukee... 42
Hall, Sylvia, one of the "Hall girls", ages of ................23, 100
death of ............ 100
fainted at sight of scalp .............. 43
family of ............ 100
marriage of .......... 100

pictures of ........ 24, 101
state land gift to..... 102
Hall, William, sketch of 23
family of ............ 23
hospitality, noted .... 24
shot by Indians....... 35
Hall, Mrs. Wm., massacred ............... 34-35
Harney, Gen., U. S. officer ................. 51
Harrison, president..... 9
Hearts, human on spears 60
Henderson, Hon. John W., escape of..... 32, 35
memorial oration of... 105
Henderson, John H., settler ................. 25
Henderson, Gen. T. J., oration ............... 105
Home, longing for... 99, 101
Horicon Lake........... 63
Horn, Mr. C. L., grandson of Elder........ 6
Horn, Miss Sylvia E., grandchild of Elder. 6
Horn, Thomas S., son of Elder ............... 100
Horn, Elder W. S., sketch of ........ 99, 101
marries Sylvia Hall.. 100
picture of ........... 101
Horses stolen from settlers ................ 39
Howard, Allen, escape of 32, 35

## I.

Illinois river........... 4, 13
Indian troubles.......... 13
bands attack settlers.. 21
land claims........... 13
marriage custom...... 23
scare ................ 31
whipped by Davis..... 29
Indians: Foxes, Sacs, etc. 13
attack Davis cottage.. 33
attempt to get girls. 69
carry away Hall girls 39
conspiracy suspected.. 81
parting from Hall girls 88
refusal to ratify treaty 16
taken to Morrison's... 84
trial of for murder... 112
wrongs of ............ 16

# INDEX

## J.
| | PAGE |
|---|---|
| Jackson, President Andrew | 9 |
| Jerome, Judge Edwin, guest of Halls | 24 |
| Johnson, Gen. Albert Sydney | 9 |
| Johnson, Col. R. M., and Shabona | 108 |

## K.
Kaskaskia, mission and capital .............. 9
Kishwaukee river....... 10
Kishwaukee Trail ...... 13

## L.
La Fayette, Gen., at Kaskaskia .............. 9
Land, Indian claims to.. 13
  donated to Hall girls. 104
Landis, Judge K. M., married Winnie Eckles ................. 98
Lands, treaty as to...... 13
Lincoln, Capt. Abraham. 44
  anecdote of .......... 53
  President, at Kaskaskia ................ 9
Little Priest, Indian chief .............. 61
  as hostage .......... 87

## M.
Maple sugar, abundance. 62, 64
Marquette, Father....... 9
Marriage and civilization 25
  Indian wife purchase.. 23
Massacre, the Indian Creek .............. 31
Medary, George, Hotel of 84
Michigan, excitement in. 54
Mill, necessity in settlement .............. 25
Miller, important settler. 25
Military movements..... 51
Military Road, course of 67, 78
Militia, drunk .......... 52
Monument erected by Munson ...... 4, 103, 104

Monument erected by state .............. 104
Monuments on site of massacre .......... 4, 103
Munson, Rachel, three generations of........ 103
  burial place of........ 98
  given land .......... 103
Munson, William, sketch of ................. 95
  family of ........ 96, 97, 98
  picture of............. 96

## N.
Neighbors, helping each other ............... 25
Norris, Robert, at work on dam ............. 33
  shot by Indians....... 36

## O.
Oconomowoc river...... 10
  lakes around.......... 63
Ox-teams for breaking prairie ............. 25

## P.
Paw Paw, Shabona's village ............... 108
Pecatonica, battle of.... 92
Pensions from England. 26
Peru, home of Elder Horn ............... 100
Pettigrew, Wm., sketch of ................. 24
  baby killed by Indian. 34
  killed by Indians...... 34
  Mrs., shot in cottage.. 34
Picture of a prairie fire. 11
  Black Hawk as civilian 21
  Back Hawk as warrior 17
  Chief Shabona ....... 30
  Monuments... 4, 27, 99, 103
  Mrs. Dunavan, Mrs. Hum, Mrs. Watts, Howard Hum, Gladys Hum, Samuel Dunavan ............ 103
  Mrs. Rachel Hall Munson and son Elliott. 97

# INDEX

Mrs. W. S. Horn and the Elder .......... 101
none of Misses Hall... 7
Shabona Park ........ 37
where girls entered canoes .............. 69
William Munson, after middle life .......... 96
Wisconsin river ....... 75
tombs of Rachel and her husband ........ 99
Portage, where girls took canoes ........ 69
Pottawatomie Indians.. 13, 16, 53
Prairie breaking ....... 25
Purse for Hall girls.... 94
Pursuit of Indians ..... 44
Pypagee, Shabona's son, friend of settlers. 22, 108
Pyps, Shabona's nephew, friend of settlers. 22, 108

## Q.
Quails, plentiful ....... 12

## R.
Rabbits, abundant ..... 12
Rachel's comb, taken by Indian .............. 62
Rachel ransomed ........ 67
Ransom from Sacs ..... 66
Ratification, refusal of Indians ............. 16
Red Bird war .......... 17
Red Flag promenade... 65
Reed, John, marries Phoebe Munson ..... 98
Reed, Fannie, married to Mr. Eckles ........ 98
Religion, Indian offering 46
Religious ceremony... 65, 73
Reward offered ......... 54
payment in goods..... 89
Rivers, formation of.... 10
Road, safest to Blue Mounds ............. 68
Rock river ............. 9
rapids passed by captives ............... 63
Romance and history... 95
Royally welcomed ....... 79

## S.
Sacs claim land ......... 16
follow girls to Portage 71
danger expected ....... 77
Sauk Trail ............. 26
Scalp, double meaning of 70
Scalping victims ...... 34
Scanlan, Miss Marian, contributor ......... 7
Scanlan, Miss Gertrude, contributor .......... 7
Scott, uncle of Hall girls 91
Settlement, Davis ...... 23
Settlers attacked by Indians ................ 21
rush to Ottawa ....... 31
return to Davis settlement .............. 32
Shabona, sketch of ..... 106
abuse of by squatters. 109
cheated out of his lands ............... 109
Col. Johnson's gift ring to ............. 108
grave of ............. 40
home on Mazon creek. 110
notifies whites ...... 22, 31
Park ................. 27
Paw Paw Village of.. 108
picture of ........... 30
removal to Kansas.... 108
second notice to settlers ................ 32
tomb of .............. 110
Shaver, Delia, married to William Munson, Jr. 98
Shaver, George, married Fidelia Munson .... 97
Sod corn, first crop .... 25
Somonauk, passing headwaters .............. 40
Spotted Arm, chief .... 57
as hostage .......... 87
Springfield, state capital, 1837 ................ 9
Starved Rock State Park 9
Stillman, Major, defeat of, "Stillman's Run" 20
"Stillman's Run", rout at .......... 20, 48, 51, 52
militia undisciplined 20, 51
pursuing Indians... 20, 51
truce flag abused...... 20
Stockades, building of.. 54

# INDEX 119

|  | PAGE |
|---|---|
| Storms, rains | 31 |
| St. Louis, girls ship for. | 93 |
| Sycamore river | 10 |
| Sycamore at rising of moon | 41 |
| Sylvia Hall, one of the "Hall girls" | 6 |
| first ransomed | 66 |

### T.

| | |
|---|---|
| Taylor Gen., report to Atkinson | 51 |
| Tecumseh, Chief | 22 |
| To-qua-mee, arrest for murder | 111 |
| acquitted of murder | 112 |
| alleged confession of murder | 113 |
| Indian marriage | 23 |
| Torture, not women captives | 64 |
| Traditions proved | 7 |
| Treaty of 1804 | 13 |
| Articles | 13-16 |
| Turkeys on prairies | 12 |
| Turnips, first crop | 25 |
| Turtle Creek | 10 |
| Turtle Village | 55 |

### V.

| | PAGE |
|---|---|
| Vance, Ed., lawyer in Dakota | 98 |
| Vance, Dr. G., marries Irma Munson | 97 |

### W.

| | |
|---|---|
| Walker, Sheriff, fearless | 111 |
| Waterway, Green Bay to Prairie du Chien | 13 |
| Watts, Mrs., picture of. | 103 |
| Waubansee, friend of the whites | 30 |
| Whirling Thunder, promises assistance | 57 |
| White Crow, promises assistance | 57 |
| character and appearance | 66 |
| makes speech to girls. | 87 |
| speech at Morrison's | 57 |
| speaks English to captives | 74 |
| White Oak Springs, description of | 91, 92 |
| Whiteside with Harney. | 51 |
| finds white scalps | 50 |
| Winnebago Indians | 16 |
| "Winnebago", steamboat for St. Louis | 93 |
| Wisconsin river scenery. | 73 |
| Woods, description | 26 |

www.ingramcontent.com/pod-product-compliance
Lightning Source LLC
Chambersburg PA
CBHW050839160426
43192CB00011B/2092